100 Ways To Save

100 Ways To Save Money

Written by Winsome Duncan

100 Ways To Save Money

100 Ways To Save Money

Written by Winsome Duncan

Photographs by RMClarke Photography

100 Ways To Save Money

Published in London by The Healing Factory Publications, 2015.

Photographs by RMClarke Photography © 2014.

Front cover picture and about the author taken by Mohamed Osman-Kamara - Esselle Media & Daniel Konteh - Surge Global. Makeup by Melisha King.

Text Copyright © 2014 by Winsome Duncan
www.creditcrunchqueen.com

The moral right of the author has been asserted.

All rights reserved. No part of this book may be reproduced, stored in a retrieval system, or transmitted in any form or by any means, electronic, mechanical, photocopying, recording, public performances or otherwise, without written permission of the publisher, except for brief quotations embodied in critical articles or reviews. The workbook is for personal use only, commercial use is prohibited unless written permission and a license is obtained from the author; Winsome Duncan.

British Library Cataloguing in Publication Data: A catalogue record for this book is available from the British Library.

Library of Congress Cataloguing in Publication Data.

Front and back cover design Alexandra Daehnhardt Designs.

ISBN: 978-1-326-13890-5

Proofread by Lisa Woodford.

Edited and book layout by Winsome Duncan.

100 Ways To Save Money

Table of Contents

Dedication	6
Foreword by Bert Jukes	9
Preface	12

100 Ways To Save Money

Making the Most Out of Your Money	18
Home is Where the Heart is	27
Family Value	32
Food and Drink Alert	36
Business as Usua	47
A Comprehensive Guide	53
The Enlightened Mind-Set	62
Everyone has a Gift to Share	72
Credit Crunch Blues: True Tales of Woe	76
A Quick Start Guide to Financial Ordering and Basic Budgeting	80

Moving on After the Recession

The Story of Money	86
A to Z Guide on How to Become Self-Employed	95
Employment Guide: Work Life after Leaving Prison	119
Coping with Redundancy	133
BONUS: Crunch It Workbook	138
Epilogue	165
About the Author	170
Ixion Challenger Gold Award	173
Services	175
MPLOYME	176
RMClarke Photography	178
Contact Us	179
Useful Links	180
Study Notes	181

Dedication

This book is dedicated to Les Brown, whose ripple effect has impacted positively on my life. Les had the courage to live his life on purpose, and overcame and triumphed the obstacles in his journey.

Thank you with all my heart for helping me to understand that I too must live what is in me. You are correct Les 'It is possible'.

100 Ways To Save Money

"100 Ways To Save Money is a brilliant book, full of ingenious ideas to help you save money. But it is also more than that. Winsome Duncan is a committed campaigner for social justice and aims to change attitudes and help people become financially literate. In tough times, this is more important than ever. I thoroughly recommend this book."

MP Simon Hughes - Minister of Justice

"I liked it, it was good, fun, easy to read. You can take the ideas and implement them, and you can talk to other people about them. It's everything I think a book should be; that's why I gave it a five-star rating."

Eddie Nestor - BBC London Broadcaster

"This book is a really handy tool for anyone who wants to save money. It does not matter what your income is; reducing your expenditure is something we are all looking to do. At Pecan, we work with people with very challengingly low incomes. Any of these tips that they take up will have an immediate benefit on theirs and their families' lives.

The section on securing employment and self-employment is going to help people who are looking for work, whether currently employed or not, to move them towards their career goals. The book is written in a way that if you want to read it cover to cover you can, or just dip into the sections. It is easy to read and works for you."

Chris Price - Pecan Executive Director
www.pecan.org.uk

100 Ways To Save Money

Foreword
by Bert Jukes

If you are reading '100 Ways To Save Money', congratulations! Give yourself a pat on the back. Well done for being the captain of your ship and steering your life in right direction.

In my lifetime, I have learned that we must become problem solvers and always think solution based. My approach to life is that my cup is not just half-full; it runneth over. However, this was not always the case.

I grew up in poverty. On the streets of Glasgow, I would play with my friends, but I never fully grasped how tough we had it at home financially. Family values mean so much to me and my parents did their best by me. As I got older, I noticed a large disparity between the haves and have-nots. I started out my career doing menial jobs like being a cleaner, just to keep the lights on and provide food on the table for my loved ones. I always knew that there was more to my life than not being able to pay bills. It was at this point in my life that I began to push for greatness and strive for success and happiness.

I am a proud Scotsman who became a serial entrepreneur with several successful businesses, and it took a lot of sweat, sleepless nights, and sacrifices. Because of this experience, I firmly believe you should

100 Ways To Save Money

never let your environment or circumstances define who you want to become.

When I met Winsome Duncan at the Les Brown conference on how to become a Motivational Speaker, her smile was infectious with a warm personality, and I could see she had a gritty passion for writing books and telling her story. I knew that, with a few tweaks here and there, Winsome could position herself as one of the leading females in the United Kingdom to help tackle the high levels of unemployment.

My driver is to serve the community, so when she reached out to me, I knew I had to extend my hand to her and the life-changing work she is doing.

The A to Z guide to self-employment is great for anyone who has an entrepreneurial mindset. It gives an overview on how to set up your own business. Another great chapter is work life after leaving prison, which encompasses the myriad of job opportunities, despite having a criminal record. The 'Crunch It' workbook is ideal for individuals who want to take the next steps in their career pathways and create a one-year goal-setting plan. If you have been made redundant or would like a passive income, this workbook will help you attain that. It is a superb resource, when Winsome delivers her MPLOYME employability workshops.

I read Winsome's book in one day and quickly realised that she was onto a winning formula. At my fingertips I had over 100 clever ways to start decreasing the cost of what I spend money on and save disposable income. There is never a right time to become unemployed, and having no money can often lead to depression and low self-esteem. This book is a great read for a low-income earner, the unemployed, those who have just left prison, or single parents.

My rags to riches tale has been a labour of love. It is a real human story that I tell to inspire the millions of people I meet around the world on some of the most renowned stages. Despite growing up as working class, my businesses have made me a multi-millionaire because I was willing to follow my passion. I want to encourage you all to keep going and never give up. You are a diamond in the rough, waiting to be discovered, polished, and admired by the world.

Bert Jukes
www.littlebigshot.com

100 Ways To Save Money

Preface

Since writing the first edition of this book in October 2011, there has been a myriad of changes in the benefits system like the universal credit and bedroom tax in the United Kingdom. The government's aim is to make sure that those who have been in receipt of long term benefits are encouraged to go out, work and effectively sign off.

The powers that be are earnestly trying to weed out those individuals that take advantage of the benefits system. We witnessed an alarming rate of people who were on incapacity benefits struggle as they were automatically signed off for work if they attended an appointment at the job centre. They were deemed fit to work if they could come for an appointment. What is more interesting is that around 80% of their incapacity benefits had to be reinstated. During this process, payment of rent and council tax were stopped and families scrambled to food banks to make sure their families could eat during these times of sanctions. I now volunteer at Pecan Foodbank in Peckham and help to collect food at their supermarket campaigns. Just by establishing a connection with them, Pecan became a partner with my company MPLOYME for the employability workshops that I teach with young people. We are both passionate about the empowerment of our community.

The bedroom tax was introduced in the UK in 2013 and basically means that if you are a single person with a two-bedroom property, you would have to pay

100 Ways To Save Money

additional tax on the empty room. If you are in receipt of state benefits, you would not be able to afford this and would need to leave your property in order to downsize. Sadly, one of the consequences of the bedroom tax has meant that some people have committed suicide because they could no longer afford to stay in their family homes in which they grew up in once their children have moved out and left empty bedrooms. In the case of Stephanie Bottrill's, she left her keys and a suicide note in her neighbour's letterbox and walked out onto the motorway and was hit by a truck and died instantly. Stephanie's story is quite disturbing and not everyone has the insight to consider renting out rooms and opening their homes up to lodgers.

This book is the second edition to the original version, *'An Inner City Guide To Surviving The Credit Crunch'*. I decided to give the book a facelift by repackaging the whole product and gave it a new title. In this second book, you will see that I have painstakingly created your very own personal BONUS 'Crunch It workbook' so that you are able to take steps towards improving your circumstances. Remember being proactive is the key here. I also have some wonderful additional chapters that will help those of you who have been made redundant or have recently left prison and desire a new career. Let's not forget our brand new A to Z guide to self-employment which is designed for those who are seriously considering being their own boss!

100 Ways To Save Money is my way of speaking out and helping those who struggle on a daily basis to survive in the harsh time of this recession. This book is an unconventional, quirky, personal guide to saving your monthly wage and becoming money-savvy. I

100 Ways To Save Money

hope you find in these pages a variety of top saving tips and suggestions for your household and for the cost-effective management of your daily lives. I believe that this turbulent financial season will produce many entrepreneurial spirits, and *100 Ways To Save Money* is my contribution. All I ask is that you be open to expanding your level of consciousness and begin to think outside the mainstream box.

Lately, when I watch the television, listen to the radio or pick up a newspaper, I am bombarded by news of job losses, business liquidations, home repossessions and bankruptcies. Having absorbed all this alarming information, I find it hard to digest my food at dinnertime – I get acid fluctuation. This led me to ponder on how to produce some creative, practical ways to cushion the painful blow of inflation.

If you are reading this book, no doubt like millions of people worldwide, you are feeling the pinch of the economic meltdown. It is a shock to the system when food and fuel prices increase as your wage plateaus or in my case decreases. I have had *100 Ways To Save Money* in mind for several years; however, due to excuses and depression on my behalf, I never got around to penning it. I had to feel the explosion of the financial pressure and burden in my life before I could commit pen to paper.

Every creed, age, and gender is directly or indirectly affected by the global change in our economy. What I know is, the recession does not discriminate and evidently, it does affect the poorer class of society the hardest. If you do not know how to save or make the pennies stretch, then you are basically stuffed like last year's Christmas turkey! For example, if you are a middle-class mother who has been made redundant,

100 Ways To Save Money

you really need to be realistic and tighten your belt, as the sushi nights out are simply not going to cut it anymore. Students will know that with grant cuts and education fees on the increase, they will need to paddle ashore for their survival and financial safety.

A huge appreciation goes out to 'Mr It's Possible' himself, Les Brown. If it were not for his daily online motivation videos, I would not have had the courage to write and live what is in me! On Saturday 28th September 2013, at the Excel Centre in East London, I got to meet in person the man around town, Les Brown. He was the first to open the stage and I made it just in time to hear him speak. I sat as close to the stage as possible which was packed with thousands of business men and women. I listened silently as he talked about 'You got to be hungry if you want to win'; on that day I was hungry to meet him and present him a signed copy of my book, which he inspired me to write. As soon as he stepped off the stage I leaped through the audience like a wild, black panther and proceeded to him. The security guard tried to stop me giving him my book (*An Inner City Guide To Surviving The Credit Crunch*)however I dodged him like Neo in the Matrix and handed it straight to Les; I looked him dead in the eye and shouted over the music and said 'You inspired me to write this book, thank you' and then security whisked him away. I never saw him again after that day; however, I knew that my mission was accomplished.

I would like to thank my sister, Lydia Duncan, who spent hours on the phone listening to me spill my creative juices. You supplied me with vital information and confidence to finish this project. You are the original ideas generator, who believes dreams come true, and I loved our email conversations. A warm,

100 Ways To Save Money

toasted thank you goes out to my family and friends who have been instrumental throughout the duration of my writing process, especially my reading party who presented me with many ideas and encouraging support – thanks for believing in my vision. The celebration party is at my house!

A special thank you goes out to my Business Mentor, Lorna Stewart, who encouraged me to change the original images and have a photo shoot for this second edition. I would also like to thank Richard Clarke for bringing the chapters to life with his photographic images and for the detailed preparation in our meeting. It was a pleasure working with you, you are a guru at what you do.

To my advisor, Gwenton Sloley, your genius has inspired me to be greater and expand out of my comfort zone. I am encouraged by your strong business acumen and commitment to seeing me achieve. There would not be a second edition of this book had it not been for your ideas of inspiration. I am forever grateful.

Last but by no means least to the living God I serve, your love is infinite, I feel it every day. What a delight it is to breathe in your world, thank you for continuing to bring my gifts and talents to the surface. I love to right the wrongs of the world through my fountain pen and I am, simply because you are!

If Divine wisdom speaks to you whilst reading this book, I strongly encourage you to use the space for study notes at the back of the book. Writing will help your ideas and thoughts to become solidified. Now, I deliver my tips and suggestions to you on a golden

100 Ways To Save Money

platter for you to banquet upon until your heart is content. Take what you need and recycle the rest.

Feast well and enjoy.

Best wishes,

Winsome Duncan.

Les Brown and I at Excel centre.

100 Ways To Save Money

Making the Most Out of Your Money

100 Ways To Save Money

1. Lose the Leaky Money Mentality
What is wrong with people who feel compelled to spend their last penny? What happiness can be derived from seeing zeros in their bank account? The leaky money mentality is paralysing the world, and if you do not seek drastic change, consider yourself to always be in the red. The best way to describe this is; the money is boring a hole in their pockets and they do not feel validated until the last penny is spent. Remember, the empty purse will tell no lies.

Expel this impoverished mentality by choosing to educate yourself about money. Some people choose to stay in the dark because it is too scary for them to search for a light switch in case they stumble and fall over their debt. Take the initiative today and transform yourself into becoming financially literate. Learn to exercise restraints in this area and your bank balance will be grateful to you.

2. Bills! Bills!! Bills!!!
Even during a recession, the majority of corporate companies tend to make profits. They know their consumers will always need essential items such as food, clothing and heating; you get it? Bearing this in mind, the keyword here for you to remember is, **NEGOTIATE**! Please, plaster-of-Paris this word to your frontal lobe and remember you have obtained the money which equates to you having got the power to negotiate! I diligently arranged a 12-month contract on a special tariff with my energy company and I saved a massive £25 off my gas bill per month. Shocking isn't it?

Like many of you, I too have had to tighten my budgeting belt during the credit crunch to the point where I find it difficult to breathe at times. This

100 Ways To Save Money

means that I needed to make savvier economic decisions. I made a list of when all my utility and leisure contracts would finish. For example, pertaining to my broadband and landline phone, I rang the call centre and said I was going to terminate my contract; the Customer Service Operator practically fell over herself to give me a great deal that was not offered on their public website. Why did they do this? It is simple: my money is valuable to them and speaks volumes, and so is yours. Start putting on your negotiation hat today and call these corporate companies to bluff and engineer the outcome to benefit you. Remember to use your best poker face!

3. Spread Your Budgeting Wings
It is imperative to start a list of your income and expenditure. This will aid you in keeping track of your money and you can work out more effectively how to save the pennies. I love working in schools, because I get to learn new skills daily. Learning how to use an Excel spreadsheet to document my income and expenditure was extremely empowering. Make the effort to learn online how to budget your accounts using a spreadsheet; this will be most beneficial to you. You can budget on a weekly or monthly basis, it is your decision. Be sure to make use of the beginner's budget table at the back on page 81.

4. Become a Calculator Whizz
When shopping in the supermarket, calculate what you are purchasing as you walk through the aisles. So, when you finally arrive at the checkout, you will not get the shock of your life. Dispute the bill if it is overpriced by your calculations. Often, supermarkets do not always show the correct display prices, but by law they must give you the lower price advertised in the store.

100 Ways To Save Money

5. One Shop, Two Shop, Three Shop, Four...
Currently, tourists love visiting London because the pound has decreased in value; this means that they can purchase quality merchandise for less. My best friend Wendy, who is a successful business woman, advised me that I must check four to six shops first before I buy. Now, I am handing this information over to you. Do not be a first-time buyer, because the chances are you can buy the same product cheaper somewhere else, especially if you search online. Have a price in mind that you want to pay for a particular item and make sure you stick to it. Price comparison websites are fabulous and they do all the work for you.

6. Fabulous Comparisons
Price comparison websites are brilliant because they take the stress out of having to shop around for the cheapest prices. The first time I used this service was to buy an Internet dongle. I got a great deal and only paid £25 because a store was having a special offer. It is a worthwhile venture, taking a little time out to research the market, and believe me; your pocket will feel the benefits.

7. Online Sellers
There are several huge online sellers. You can become a merchant and sell duplicate gifts, new or slightly used household items that you no longer require. Make sure your product is in good condition as consumers are able to rate your product and offer feedback. There is a small administrative fee for uploading items. Use the instruction guide or ask a friend who uses online sellers regularly for a tutorial.

8.The Boot is in the Car
When having a major de-clutter, you may find that

there are bags of items that you have grown out of. There is money to be made in car boot sales' ventures. Products are usually sold between 50p and £5, so you will not become a millionaire. However, you will be on the path to earning an extra income. This is a superb way to improve your sales negotiations skills as discussed in tip 2, Bills! Bills!! Bills!!! Make sure you arrive at your pitch on time so you can maximise your selling potential.

9. It is not the Pawn on a Chess Board

The dreaded pawnshop can be a great place to make some extra cash if you have broken gold lying around the house. If you are not going to use these items, then you might as well get some money for it instead of it sitting dormant. Pawning your own jewellery is another story. Be warned that many get caught out because of the astronomical 114% interest charges you have to repay on full term contracts. If you have problems paying back current debts, what makes you think that you are going to pay off these items any quicker? Scrap gold, yes; pawning jewellery you own, that's up to you!

10. Find a Copper

Pennies turn into pounds and pounds are great friends with fifty pound notes, and those red-face folks are in the company of millionaires. Let's face it, times are extremely hard. I get a headache just thinking about managing from pay cheque to pay cheque. Whatever I can do to improve my financial situation, I will endeavour with every part of my being. I play a game called 'find a copper'. The streets of London are not paved with gold; however, you can spot loose, homeless change in between the cracks of the pavements if you look really carefully. Feel no shame bending down and claiming your penny, then keep on

100 Ways To Save Money

walking. If you are that paranoid about people watching you, pretend you are tying your shoelace and scoop that copper up and step.

I have watched young people on several occasions just dash their pennies in the street and laugh. The joke is ultimately on them, their disrespectful attitude for their money will rear its ugly head when they are in a long line at the Job Centre signing on. Save all your loose change in a jar for a year and then cash that baby in!

11. A Discipline Logbook
I admit that in the beginning when I started keeping a manual paper log of my daily expenditure, I would work with inaccurate, estimated figures. With time and practice, I have learned to log everything down that I buy and with patience, I am learning to keep accurate records. I do find this challenging; however, I am willing to do what it takes to improve my financial situation.

12. Save £91 Instantly
It makes no sense to pay £1.75 to take out your money from an automated teller machine that charges you to use it. Think about it this way; if you were to use this method of cash withdrawal on a weekly basis, by the end of the year you would have spent £91. Walk the extra mile to another ATM and withdraw your money for free.

13. Automatic Protection
When you bravely signup for a credit card, be sure to read the fine print, because many people get caught out with additional charges unbeknownst to them. Once the ink has dried, many credit card companies

will automatically take a monthly automated protection payment. You do have an opt-out clause and this could save you hundreds of pounds per annum if you use it.

14. In it to Win it
Here is the deal: you can save money every year by not playing the lottery, or you can take a risk and gamble on the fact that you might win. Here is an interesting fact; in the UK, you have a one in 14 million chance of winning the lottery. It is a catch-22 baby – you decide!

15. There Will Be Rainy Days
Save 10% of your income and do not touch it; let that money grow and gain interest. It is a great feeling knowing you have a comfort cushion to fall back on during emergencies. Saving money regularly is a fantastic way of becoming financially independent and demonstrates discipline. Just so we are clear, going to get your hair done, your fingernails manicured or purchasing the latest boy toy is not classified as an emergency!

16. Poverty Consciousness
Now is the time to examine your impoverished beliefs. I come from a working-class family, so anything I wanted, my father would have to budget and save up for it. He always told me to save for a rainy day. I did not realise that there would be many rainy days in my life. I never listened to him and paid the consequences dearly by getting into copious amounts of debt. I have had to retrain myself to think and believe that money flows to me in abundance. It has not been easy to change rooted childhood beliefs and is still a work in progress. The more I practice feeling good about myself, the more abundant I become.

100 Ways To Save Money

17. Become Financially Independent
Break new ground and do something you have never done before. Imagine someone whose life is more famous than yours. Let's take Oprah Winfrey for example; she found her passion through the medium of commercial television and proceeded to have a number one, prime time talk show worldwide. Oprah's success is based on finding what she was good at and mastering her craft. You can become financially independent and debt-free as long as you do not limit your capabilities.

18. Credit That Keeps You Debt-Free
Pay-as-you-go credit cards are a superb way for paying online when you have a poor credit history and banks have declined your loan application. You will never have to worry about being in the red and you have the freedom to get your wages paid into this credit card account. The only drawback is a small registration cost and you will need to pay a fee for using the card per item or on a monthly basis. Choose the price plan best suited for you and think about how frequently you will use the card.

19. A Wise Voicemail Tells a Cost-Saving Message
I relish this tip as it is a personal favourite of mine, because I love to think outside the box. When I purchased my new phone and contract, I was charged outside of my monthly minute allowance after a client left me a voicemail. I receive a high volume of calls, and discovered towards the end of the month that my minutes had finished and I was unable to collect my voicemails. This was due to an extortionate call charge rate of 50 pence per minute. What kind of business could I operate without direct contact to my clients? Maybe 'a joke business'.

I also owned a pay-as-you-go phone that offered free voicemail all year round. The light bulb went off in my head and in a flash, I diverted my contract calls to transfer to my business number with free voicemail and collected all of my messages. It saves me approximately 45 talk-time minutes per month, which is a huge difference in air time saving.

20. Making Money While You Sleep
In order to participate in financial freedom, you need to create a residual income. When you have a nine-to-five job, you are limited to what the company offers to pay you. When you arrive at your maximum pay scale, what then? I understand not everyone has the creative direction to become a CEO; however, you really need to earnestly find ways in which you can earn money while you sleep. I would like you to consider the potential of creating an extra, monthly, passive income which means you can earn money 24 hours a day, seven days a week. You can do this in the following ways:

- Music royalties
- Book publishing
- Renting out properties
- Online services
- As a private product distributor

These are only a few options; be sure to research online for the best income suited for you.

100 Ways To Save Money

Home is Where the Heart is

100 Ways To Save Money

21. Friendly Worms
You will be hearing a lot about the 99p shops, since that is the place to be when cash is absent without leave. These stores are usually recognisable by their bright, neon yellow and red signs. The good 99p shops will be filled to the brim with these worms. What on God's green earth is a friendly worm? It is oblong in shape, it is made out of thick, fibre material stuffed with a cotton-wool type filling and is approximately the width of your door. It is a draught-excluder, and it is a wonderful way to keep warm at home during winter. If you are handy with the sewing machine, you can make one yourself by purchasing the material and stuffing from the market. Walk around your home and count the number of doors that touch the floor. If, for example, you have five doors, then purchase the same amount of friendly worms.

22. Soapy Issues
WARNING!! Inspiration lives here: the following tip is what gave me the idea to write my book. When you find that your bathroom soap dispenser is running low, add the same amount of water as the remaining soap liquid, shake the container viciously and give it a test squeeze. Granted, the soap liquid will be a thinner consistency, however, you can be reassured that it will last until next payday or until someone loans you the money to buy some more. The same rule applies for washing up liquid. Hey, it is worth a try.

23. Can't Wash or Can't Afford to Wash?
Surprise, not everyone has the luxury of a washing machine in their homes. Some people have to get on a bus, walk or ride a bike to their local launderette. The impact of this cost is £6 – £10, depending on if

100 Ways To Save Money

you spin dry or use the tumble dryer. What do you think people did before they had washing machines? Yes, you have guessed it, they washed by hand and the last time I checked, it is still an effective method. Honestly speaking, you can save money in this area - you cannot say I did not educate you! Do not allow your Western reliance on machinery to close your mind to this fabulous suggestion. Get back to your roots and save money, honey.

24. Netting Benefits
A simple way to retain heat in your home is to exclude draughts by purchasing netting for underneath your curtains. This is a great cost-effective way to keep in extra warmth, leaving cold air where it should be; outside.

25. Simply Unplug
Leaving the television, digital viewing box or stereo on standby uses almost the same amount of electricity as if it was turned on. By unplugging your electrical equipment at night, you will save on your monthly bills.

26. Boiling Point
When making a hot drink, make sure you only use the correct amount of water. If you are boiling a full kettle of water for one cup of tea, you are wasting your electricity. You can amass a fortune in savings when you become aware of excess power use.

27. To Burgle or Not to Burgle?
If you are going aboard, you can buy a special timer plug that turns electrical appliances on and off at your scheduled time. This gives the illusion of your property being occupied in your absence. This deters

burglars and saves you money by not having to replace your stolen items.

28. To Heat or Not to Heat, That is the Question?

Always make sure you have a spare electric heater as a backup during the winter nights. You do not want to get caught on the wrong side of the snow. I remember a freezing November when the snow roared an ivory song. My central heating broke down and it took three days to fix it; but lucky for me, I used my heater and had one warm room at home, for which I was genuinely grateful.

Avoid fan heaters as they use excessive wattage and cut out frequently. Instead, invest in a 20-inch, upright heater with legs, for which prices start from a reasonable £19.99. Do not get caught out with an ice rink-theme heating system.

29. Brush Your Teeth

It was also this second tip which inspired me to write *'100 Ways To Save Money'* which is the first edition of this book. I thought to myself: 'wouldn't it be useful if we had handy tips like this in a book'. Here is what happened; one bright, early morning I awoke to enter the bathroom, and to my dismay, I had finished my toothpaste. What is a lady to do? I was in a rush as per usual and I did not have time to go to the shops. Then the light bulb turned on in my head and said cut the end of the toothpaste tube and scrape it on to my toothbrush. There was no need to walk around with a smelly mouth after all. Remember you can do the same for hand cream tubes as well.

100 Ways To Save Money

30. Make a Needle Your Best Friend
This year, it is all about sew and repair. I am learning to use a needle and thread when my clothes have holes instead of throwing them away. Most of my wardrobe is loose-fitting due to my weight-loss journey. When I need to create a new outfit, it is about mix and match, and I am now getting into my sewing groove. Try it, do not be shy.

31. Second-hand is Back in Demand
There is nothing wrong with second-hand goods. In fact, you would be doing the environment a favour by recycling more. Be careful when purchasing second-hand electrical goods, as they do not usually come with a guarantee. When buying furniture, look out for any signs of possible bug infestations. Small, brown spots are signs of bed bugs.

32. Free Furniture
We are living in a 'consumer age' where people have more than they need. It is a travesty when so much goes to waste in the world today. I was walking with my friend to her car, when she noticed four chairs with black cushions, sitting outside all alone. There was nothing wrong with them, I just needed to give them a good scrub with bleach and soap once they got home. Minutes later, we got to her car and there we saw a medium-sized mirror on the floor, laying there abandoned. Again, there was nothing wrong with it. On the same day we both found items to reuse for our benefit. There are fantastic websites that will help you exchange furniture for free: go and search online. I wrote this book you are reading on a black, wooden office desk, which I found for free outside my home. You go figure it out!

100 Ways To Save Money

Family Value

100 Ways To Save Money

33. Abstinence is the Key
I have not yet been blessed with children, so I decided to ask my friends who have children what their top money-saving tips would be. The first text response I received was from a long-term, secondary school friend. It read, 'Don't have children'! I found this hilarious – remember ladies and gentleman, sexual abstinence could save you a wad of cash.

34. Getting to Grips With the Figures
Learn financial literacy by sticking to your budget. You do not need to dress your children in designer outfits, as they will tear, soil and damage their clothing easily. Remember tip 3, Spread Your Budgeting Wings? The same rules apply.

35. Use a Present Twice
I adore mums who are inventive; it warms my heart. Many gift-wrapped presents come with huge bows attached to them. On one occasion, a yummy mummy I know decided that she would make a hairband with her daughter, using a bow from a previous present. They did this by simply attaching a ribbon to it. This is a great parent/child bonding moment. How cute is that?

36. Pasta Toys
I believe that teachers have one of the best professions in the world. They possess the power to change the direction of a child's life. Especially with all of the government cuts happening at present, teachers still get pupils through their exams. I use to work in a school and asked a male colleague, 'How do you provide fun activities when the family has no money?' He replied, 'We would make toy dolls and paint pasta shells for necklaces and bracelets'. How cool is that?

37. Free Stuff and Preparation
Let's face it, children are expensive because they grow each year. We are in a climate where prices have soared, yet, your wage remains the same. As a parent, what are you expected to do? You can search online or look at the newspapers for free children's activities. You can feed the ducks in the park or visit free museums. Take the time to make sure you prepare a packed lunch, as this will save you digging into your pocket for money to buy crisps, drinks and snacks throughout your day. Enjoy.

38. The Big Freeze
When you buy your meat in bulk, make sure you section it out into portions and freeze it. This way, you will be able to ration how much you need to use throughout the month for family meals.

39. For a Fiver
Feed your family for a fiver. Challenge yourself, you can do it. Make a fun, cheap meal for four. You can make a vegetable noodle stir fry, barbecue chicken with rice and peas, or have spaghetti Bolognese. You can even fit in an apple pie for dessert if you know how to handle your money correctly. This is a great credit-crunching challenge, get the children involved and help improve their maths.

40. Free Meals
It is rare; however, some restaurants still advertise deals such as children under ten can eat for free. Hunt out that eatery for special occasions like birthdays or anniversaries and make a fun family outing.

41. The Pool
All yummy mummies need to get together and

100 Ways To Save Money

create a babysitting pool. This will save huge amounts of money when you want to paint the town red. A word of caution: be sure your sitter is trustworthy, as far too often we hear of so many cases of child abuse

100 Ways To Save Money

Food and Drink Alert

100 Ways To Save Money

42. Economy Price
I am not ashamed to tell you that my trolley is packed to the brim with smart price products and special deals. I nearly fell over when I went into my regular superstore and discovered that their smart price tissues went up from 31p to 54p, which is over one-third of the original product price. I find this leap in economy prices worrying, so imagine how much more brand names products have increased. Please note, it is a great idea to shop at the less popular mainstream stores. You will pay much less for non-brand items. I have been known to spend £20 in these stores and have accumulated half a trolley's worth of shopping. It is simply super fantastic for your pantry and well worthwhile. The only drawback is you have to purchase bags; this is so the store can keep their costs down. I always get around this by bringing my own bags or trolley.

43. No Frills Please, We're British!
I love a bargain. However, this means I still have to test-check my no frills products. For example, I bought a tin of economy baked beans for 9p many moons ago and the beans tasted like hard pellets, the sauce was of a thin consistency, and it had little tomato flavouring. There is no point in buying economy products which you will not eat. You have got to know how to play it smart. The compromise here was to buy the no frills spaghetti. No frills products are great trolley-fillers and are substantially more cost-effective. Anything that says 'smart value', 'saver', 'smart price' or 'economy quality' is a walk in the right direction. Question: Did you know being able to range from no frills apple juice to sushi temaki hand-rolls is an art? I call it ghetto chic!

100 Ways To Save Money

44. BOGOF
Buy one get one free (also known as BOGOF) can save you loads of dosh, but remember some superstores do have a cap on these deals, such as six items per customer. In case you are wondering, I used to work in retail and I know some of the abbreviations used. Make sure you only purchase special deals when you need them.

45. A Special Delivery on Price
Always look out for any in-store promotions. I have been blessed with this knack of walking into a food store whilst pondering what is on my shopping list and finding wonderful offers to match. To my surprise, there are at least one or two deals on my list that I grab and take advantage of. For example, I wanted to get some blackcurrant squash which you dilute with water to drink. Right in front of me was a neon yellow label saying £1 only! Granted, it was strawberry flavour but I am on the right track by making a compromise with a brand-name product.

46. The Value of a Voucher
Collect store loyalty cards or discount vouchers for products from magazines and newspapers, and use them in your weekly shop. Remember to purchase products that you will use. Be mindful of the voucher expiration date; I have been frequently caught out at the checkout with expired vouchers staring blankly into the cashier's face. This is accompanied by my flushed, rosy cheeks that are slightly embarrassed.

47. Super Reductions
Just in case you did not know, a supermarket's goal is to make profit. At the end of the working day, they would rather reduce items than to log them off as shrinkage. Look out for what reductions are on offer

100 Ways To Save Money

and freeze your perishable goods on the day if necessary.

48. The Warehouse
Shopping in bulk at your local wholesalers will save you large portions of money. Make sure you get up early when travelling to fish or meat markets. You can go with a friend and share the cost. Remember to bring the car or a shopping trolley to carry your heavy load.

49. Market Value
I wish I could write this tip on your forehead in black, permanent ink so you can remember; market prices are cheaper than superstores because they have less packaging. When you purchase your fruits and vegetables, obtain the newest produce. What can tend to happen is traders want to clear their old stock first, which could mean that you arrive home and notice that some of the food has already spoiled or is turning mouldy. The key here is to make sure you are getting value for money all round. Go and support your local Sole Trader.

50. Make Restaurants Work For You
In this climate of recession, businesses have to become more creative to tantalise the public's taste-buds and sustain profits. I have been enticed by 2-for-1 offers, eat as much as you like, or pay £9.99 for a 2-course meal or £12.99 for a 3-course meal with a beverage of your choice. Research the best deals online or ask friends and family what their recommendations are. I love seafood and sushi, which admittedly is quite expensive; therefore, this becomes an occasional treat. However, when clients want to take me out, guess where I want to go? To a sushi bar, yes please!

100 Ways To Save Money

51. Eat, Eat, Eat
Eat as much as you like is a fantastic offer and value for money; look around for the best deals. Buffets start as low as £4.99 which is a cheap night out and an effective way of budgeting. I am not an advocate of gorging anymore, so I suggest you know your limits when food is plentiful and in abundance. What is the point of feeling stuffed and sluggish after a meal? Please note that people who eat at buffets are more likely to consume 30% more food.

52. Nothing is For Free
Be very careful not to be enticed by 'free' offers. Shops in general have a clever way of marketing to make you feel you are getting something for nothing. Remember this is the credit crunch and they are making back money through other products throughout the store especially close to the checkouts or on open-end shelves.

53. The Impulse To Stay Broke
Avoid impulse-buying and become aware of mind control tools that are in place to make you part with your hard-earned cash.

54. Likky Likky People
The terminology 'Likky Likky' is Jamaican patois; it means one who is greedy about eating everything that is seen. Some folks have a bottomless pit for a belly and can easily drain your supplies by eating you out of house and home. You know the type, they do not spend their money on anything, however, they are happy to eat most of your pantry. Here is a simple solution for when Mr or Mrs Likky Likky stops by for a bite to eat; give them one serving only or not at all. Yes, you read correctly, you have a right to refuse a

100 Ways To Save Money

second helping and to use the word 'no' in your vocabulary. Learning to say the word 'no' takes practice, but is worth it; you are not being rude, you are setting a boundary. Think about it, would you rather have a little extra for yourself and your family or would you prefer to see a hungry night? Take your pride out of the picture and keep it real.

55. Food Banks
Sadly, many people now find themselves on the tightrope of poverty during this economic crisis. If you find yourself below the poverty line, you really have to pool all your resources and get your pride out the way. Food banks can help you feed your family on a short-term basis, when the cupboards are bare and cash is non-existence. They normally supply three days' worth of food. Food banks operate solely on donations from the public, if you are in a position to give dried/canned foods or money please do. I partnered up with www.pecan.org.uk to help their clients back into work. I also volunteer there in my spare time.

56. Half a Cup of Tea Please
My adopted granny gave me another wonderful tip when drinking tea. Did you know you can make tea twice with one bag? Simply use the bag twice before adding milk. You can also double a pint of full fat milk by adding a pint of water. Now you have skimmed milk for your cereal and tea.

57. Get Your Drink On
I do not consider myself to be the world's greatest party animal. However, several of my friends and associates tend to go out to town frequently. If you and your friends are planning a night out, grab a couple bottles of wine or a 6-pack of beer from the

supermarket. Gather everyone around a couple of hours prior and get your drink on before you hit the club.

58. I Will Have the Tap Water Please!
When dining out, order a jug of premium, government tap water with ice. If you want to be fancy, ask for slices of lemon to accompany your beverage. This is a great way of saving £2–£9 on soft drinks and an even bigger saving if you are drinking alcohol. Do not worry about being perceived as cheap; you now have to keep it real with your purse or wallet. I know of an oriental restaurant in Brixton (South London) that charges 20p per glass of water; overall, it is still a huge saving. Remember the penny is related to the pound, the pound has connections to fifty red-faced friends in high places, and that is not to mention their links to a millionaire's mind-set! By the way, has anyone seen a hundred dollar bill?

59. Grandma's Chicken Feet
I am a lucky lady to have three grannies. The one that told me about this winter soup recipe is my adopted granny. I remember we were chatting on the phone one freezing evening; well, let's face it, Britain is hardly warm. Granny was in sun-soaked Barbados while I was in icy London. She said, you can go to the butchers and buy a bag of chicken feet for £1.99. When you get home, wash the chicken feet in lemon and salt water and then make a couple of incisions in the legs so the juice can come out easily and make the soup become thicker. You boil the chicken feet up into a broth, and then add vegetables and seasonings to taste. You can use potatoes, leeks, carrots or any of your favourite vegetables. I have never tried this soup, however, I do know people who do eat offal that was formerly known as slave food. Times are

100 Ways To Save Money

hard right? It is what it is – you decide! This year I am going to challenge myself and make a YouTube video for this soup - look out for it in 2014.

60. Black Baked Beans
You must teach yourself to bulk up on your mealtimes. When cooking salt fish or canned goods like salmon, tuna or corn beef, add vegetables to increase the volume of the dish. Excellent food bulkers are sweet corn, cabbage or pulses. By making the meal more plentiful, you can feed more people. My fondest childhood food memory was corn beef and cabbage on a bed of rice. Feel free to experiment.

Black baked beans is a favourite recipe of mine; this dish is a great breakfast delight. Remember we discussed the idea of using vegetable as a bulking agent? Fry up two medium-sized onions in a pan until slightly soft, add black pepper, a knob of butter, a hint of hot pepper sauce for flavour. Then add the tin of baked beans and heat it all up together. It is absolutely delicious. I call it black baked beans because it is spicy and in the Caribbean we love spice.

61. The Joy of Becoming a Veggie Eater
The last time I checked, lentils and other pulses were still cheaper than meat and are a wonderful source of protein. Taking this into account, surely the logical answer to saving money is to become a vegetarian. The benefits are you will be healthier, as meat can take up to 72 hours to digest in our bodies and when it gets lodged in our intestines it becomes putrid. Remember most supermarkets use water and chemicals in their meat products to increase the buying weight. If you do not believe me, go online and research it for yourself. You may even lose a

couple of pounds with a healthy living diet, which can be a great confidence-builder for you.

62. Save the Soul Food

In most Caribbean cultures, it is traditional when at parties you to take some food back home with you. Soul food is cooked and prepared with love and goes down a treat. I always ask the host's permission to take food home; although, they usually offer. I then wrap up that jerk chicken in foil or scoop coleslaw into a cup and make a speedy exit. The same rule applies at work functions, providing your boss gives you the go ahead; do eat plentifully and take some food home. Beware of leakages and remember paper plates, foil or cling film are perfect carriers for those delicious bites.

63. Finger-Licking Good

When my schedule is particularly overloaded, I do not get the time to cook as often as I would like. In this instance, I visit my favourite Caribbean takeaway and purchase barbecue jerk chicken from the charcoal grill. When the recession kicked in, the price for a small portion of jerk chicken went up from £2.50 to £3.50. My budget was tight and I decided to opt for the oven-cooked small portion at £1.50, this is a saving of £2.00. It is a big difference, and my pocket and my belly appreciated it. I still get to taste the spicy flavour of the Caribbean at a fraction of the cost.

64. A Hot Expert

I am a total fan of do-it-yourself wherever and whenever possible. A friend suggested to me that I should try looking at the ingredients of hot pepper sauce and make my own version. I thought this was a great idea as I love being creative and I added my

100 Ways To Save Money

own variation such as ginger and Celtic salt. My recipe worked wonders and, for the past two years, I have made my own hot pepper sauce and given it to friends and family who adore it. Not only have they requested repeat orders, but they have also expressed interest in me bottling up the sauce. Since then, I have gone on to make barbecue sauce and fish seasoning, which has not only saved me money but it is also tastier then the corporate store version. When I get a lucrative investor to support my range, I will create my own line of Caribbean sauces.

65. Grow it
There is something so peaceful about making contact with the earth. I find it quite relaxing. If you have a garden, try growing your own organic fruits and vegetables. Those without a garden can grow cress in a small pot indoors and add it to your salads.

66. Spice it Up
Homemade popcorn is a fantastic snack and a low-cost replacement for brand-name crisps. My favourite seasoning is to add a dash of Cajun spice. More recently, I tried jerk seasoning flavour and it was just as delicious. Popcorn has a much lower percentage of fat than standard crisps and I use it to aid my weight loss.

67. Two Left Gloves
There must be a hidden claw in my right hand, because when I am washing up the dishes, I always tear the right hand glove first. This is seriously annoying and leaves me with three to four stacks of left hand gloves. I replace the glove which has a hole as opposed to opening a brand new packet. I remembered on one occasion, I kept forgetting to put washing up gloves on my shopping list for a whole

week. When I got home in the evening, the dishes needed to be cleaned. What is a lady in distress to do? The light bulb went off in my head; I thought: use two left hand gloves to wash up. Granted, it is a very uncomfortable experience, however, at least I did not have a stack of dirty, smelly dishes piling up. My mother always told me, 'Make do with what you have'.

100 Ways To Save Money

Business as Usual

100 Ways To Save Money

68. Say No to Viruses
I am always on the lookout for new ways to improve on saving money, especially as I work part-time and live in London which is one of the most expensive capitals in the world. There are several free antivirus software on the Internet, however, they do not offer full protection like the ones customers pay for. Consider this; a variety of local government authorities store highly sensitive information within their technology networks. This means they have extensive anti-virus software licences for multiple computers which can extend to cover staff computers at home. You can call it the perks of the job. Contact your IT support today and confirm if this offer can extend to you. That way, you will be getting a free, top of the range anti-virus software service.

69. The Art of Exchanging Services
This is a great way of collective teamwork. My friend happens to be an electrician. My stereo is over a decade old and it decided to stop working and started spinning my CD deck continually. The electrician wanted an updated biography for his website and I wanted my stereo fixed, so we did a straightforward, easy swap of services. Remember, this principle can be used for swapping clothes with friends or giving away clothes that you no longer wear, instead of them sitting dormant. Trade by barter is good and a friend in need is a friend indeed.

70. Conferences and Seminars
Take advantage of FREE conferences and seminars that pertain to your working field. This is a fantastic way of networking and connecting with people from all around the world during the credit crunch. These mammoth opportunities need to be milked for what they are worth. If you are really lucky, some of these

100 Ways To Save Money

functions provide delicious canapés or light refreshments. You must have the confidence, or at the very least act like you have confidence, to open your mouth and speak about your talents, skills and the services that you have to offer. Remember, practice makes perfect.

71. Product Sellers
If you are an artist selling your merchandise, always aim to sell your product especially if your intellectual property is involved. Often, some people can tend to demand items for free or as trade-off for their products. Only trade if the product is worthwhile and beneficial to you. Be shrewd in business; it is not about making friends here or massaging egos. If you are not good at sales, then learn now that your objective is to increase your profit margin.

72. Ink it
If you are like me and use your printer frequently, buying new ink cartridges can be a costly business. Currently, many brand-name printer ink cartridges can be extortionate, especially when several modern cartridges are chipped and are no longer refillable. Shop around; there are companies that supply non-brand versions of the same ink cartridges for a fraction of the price and can save your pounds in the months to come. Prices start from £5 upwards and of course you could get a discount for a full set. If you are lucky enough to own a printer that still has injectable ink refills, then make sure you purchase economy inks for approximately £4.99, and get refilling.

73. Black Ink
When the struggle is at its peak in the office, I only use black ink to print out my work. This saves me

having to buy 3 other colours and I can still get the job done. Another great tip is to use draft print-outs for non-public documents in order to save ink.

74. Internationally Connected
Calling cards are a fantastic, cost-effective way to connect with loved ones and business contacts internationally. But beware of the daily deductions fees once you start making calls: some cards deduct up to 25p a day with connection fees added per call made. My personal favourite when connecting with friends abroad is online video calls. It is not free, however, it will be included in your monthly Internet billing and has a personal touch.

75. International Texts
Being the entrepreneur that I am, means I communicate with my clients all over the world. One thing I am mindful of is that international texts cost me double the price to send. Wherever possible, I try my upmost hardest to keep everything I have to say in one text or in 160 characters, and I frequently use abbreviations to be concise.

76. Entertainment Showcases
Nowadays, many bars and clubs are closing down because they cannot sustain a substantial amount of punters. More and more business owners have to create a strategic plan to attract a drinking crowd. For us this means free admittance to plush, West End nightclubs. Clubs tend to make the majority of money on the bar and will open their doors to entertainment showcases and promoters who have huge followers.

77. Pick it Up
Being an Event Promoter means you can accumulate a high volume of expenditure. For an entertainment

event, my business partner and I would purchase 5,000 A6 flyers and distribute them at live showcases. Not everyone is interested in our particular style of event and some only take a flyer to be polite. At the end of the night, we will find a few flyers on the floor, chairs or tables. We would scan the venue to collect left-over flyers that are not wet. You have to remember that the unit cost of one flyer is 16 pence and our business needs to save every penny.

For our very first event more than nine years ago, we could not afford 5,000 flyers to promote it. I came up with the idea of printing our event details on small business cards to save money and get the word out. It worked! I printed up 300 business cards on a sky-blue background and we had a sold-out 3S.T.Y.L.E event. Condensation was on the windows that night and people stood outside because there was no room to get in. 3S.T.Y.L.E was an improvised, artistic expression which meant free, successful, talented, young lyrical engineers. You can view our classic video footage online. As an entrepreneur, you must be bold, inventive and create a path where previously overgrown weeds once lived. Do what you can to get by until you become successful.

78. Embracing Another Skill

You can make more money in life by learning an extra trade; do not allow yourself to be boxed in. Education is the key and in this current unstable climate, you must take advantage of every opportunity that can further your career. There are some decent companies out there that are still willing to invest in their employees, despite the economic downturn. Take full advantage of their educational offers beneficial to you. I have been offered an opportunity to study a diploma in specialist learning support free of charge. Needless to say, I graciously accepted with open arms. Equip yourself with as much educational ammunition as possible.

79. Free Tools For Your Business
I really adore this tip; in fact, it makes me tingle all over. If you are a new business or an artist desiring to raise your profile, then you must become business-savvy and start sharing your brand today! Yes, you can create your own website using FREE templates online. How fantastic is that? Please, note you will have their website name attached to your site in order to promote their brand and get in customers for them. This is how they make their money. Some people will say it looks unprofessional, however I disagree because everyone has to start somewhere. It is the beginning of your foot being placed firmly on the ladder of recognition. Please note there are opportunities to purchase your own domain name from these template sites. When I never had a website I created an online fan page to promote my services and get my message out there.

100 Ways To Save Money

A Comprehensive Guide

100 Ways To Save Money

80. Build a Great Rapport
On this road called life, you never know when you will need to call in a favour. It costs nothing to be courteous to your local pharmacist, kebab shop or local corner shop. You may fall on a slender day with a hungry belly and you may need that prescription, 10p off your bag of chips or an understanding Customer Service Manager, when you discover that the smart price baby wipes marked up at the till is now £1.49 when actually the price tag reads £1. Remember the tip, 'become a calculator whizz'? By law, shops have to sell a product at the price displayed otherwise it is false advertising. Did I mention that I have worked in retail?

81. Ask – Borrow – Smile
Desperate times call for desperate measures whilst living in the credit crunch. I encourage you to ask for what you want. If you do not ask, you will not get and please, for goodness sake, do not presume other people become mind-readers and automatically know what you want. I am sure each individual can think for themselves without your mental projections. Ask politely to borrow a cup of sugar if you have to; fundamentally, this borrowing mentality perpetuates the poverty cycle. However, everyone needs a cup of tea to chase away the blues; well, at least my mum does. The lesson here is not to perceive yourself as a leech, but view it as you have stumbled on hard times and need a helping hand. Smile to those that cross your path to help you; it costs you nothing and could make your day.

82. Homemade vs. Superstore
I am a creative person and I produce homemade cards, framed poetry and gifts. I have saved money using my hub of creativity by utilising my skills and

100 Ways To Save Money

talents to create unique pieces of artwork. This is a fantastic original way of making presents and is a million times more sentimental in its value than any corporate gift on a superstore shelf.

83. Pass on the Present
This tip is a precarious one. Some people are of the mind-set that it is rude to give away presents that you have received. However, I believe this is a personal choice. If you have got a substantial collection of bubble bath, soaps, perfumed products or duplicated gifts, do not hoard them, pass it on. Remember the trick here is how you can save money, honey. Warning: make sure you do not give a present to the same person that gave it to you. How embarrassing would that be?

84. Walk this Way
Try walking instead of taking the bus for a 10-15 minute journey. You will improve your fitness levels and save money at the same time. The mind is like a light bulb, it works best when switched on. I have been known to power walk for up to 90 minutes, which is approximately five miles.

85. Get on the Bus
You can get anywhere in London using the bus. Granted, it will probably take you two to three times longer than the train, however, get on the bus when all else fails. Let's face it, traffic is often variable and roadworks can cause delays, however, it means you can save at least £10 or more per month depending on your travel zones.

86. Working all Hours
If you work full-time and are finding it challenging to cover priority bills, try looking for a second part-time

evening or weekend job. This can provide some much needed grocery shopping or spending money. This is a short-term solution as you do not want to head down the road of exhaustion.

87. The Salesman Knocks 10 Million Times
Are you bombarded with landline sales calls? Make your number ex-directory. Over the years, when I received these annoying calls, I learnt to firmly refuse them by saying 'No thank you'. Saying a strong 'no' means you get to keep your money in your pocket.

88. Switch Off
Once upon a time, I could afford the luxury of a car. I remember cruising around London with my tank of petrol on empty. On the odd occasion, I have been a witness to traffic jams that will not move because of major roadworks or an accident. I figured that if I was to sit in stationary traffic, it made sense to switch the engine off. It was either that or run out of petrol. During that period of my life, money was non-existent, regardless of the fact I was in full-time employment.

89. Ahh-Chou
I suffer from hay fever and one fine summer's day, I got caught at the bus stop without tissues and with a streaming nose. I was about to spend 40p on a packet of tissues from the shop. However, knowing I had a multi-pack at home or I could go to the pound store and purchase 10 pocket packs of tissues for £1, instead I politely asked a mother with two children if she had any spare tissues. She gave me two and this carried me to my next destination. If you are too shy to ask in person, pop into your local fast food restaurant or supermarket and use the tissues in the toilets.

100 Ways To Save Money

90. Get Rid of the Box
If you are not an avid TV watcher, Internet user, or do not possess an Android phone, then what is the point in paying for a TV licence? You could save yourself approximately £145.50 annually by not having a TV licence. You can use the spare money to go on a short break, buy a book or go on a nature hike.

91. Unemployed and Afraid
Having had a direct experience of what it feels like to be unemployed after being made redundant, I can tell you it really broke my spirit and self-confidence. I ended up in more debt trying to survive. This may alarm you, however, you must realise that looking for work is a full-time job which you must pursue fiercely, be under no illusion about that. My friend Denise who worked in marketing would say to me, 'Make sure you are filling out at least five applications per week'.

The best technique is to have a strong curriculum vitae (CV) and personal statement, then copy and paste into applications which will save you time. Brush up on your interview responses by role-playing with a friend. You may need to improve on your academic skills as well, so look into further education or government training schemes so that you have a better advantage than the other candidates. Be an expert in your field of work and have a positive mental attitude to all your interviews. Remember, embracing another skill can secure you your dream job.

92. A Holiday in 24 Hours
Save a bundle of cash by booking last minute holidays a couple of days in advance. Be prepared to leave promptly. The wait at the airport can sometimes be

time-consuming if you are waiting for cancellations on the day of travelling.

93. 0% Commission
When travelling abroad, I always visit my local Post Office. They provide me with 0% commission on foreign currency exchange. I practically skip into the premises and I am so happy to avoid 2%-plus charges at independent booths.

94. Outlandish Hairstyles
Be creative, adventurous and economic with your hairstyles. Number one: take a serious look at how much money you spend on the latest hairstyles. Number two: realistically think about how you can cut back the cost; for example, washing your hair yourself instead of getting a salon to do it. Number three: if you have afro hair, you can learn to plait your own hair or twist it. Do not try and trim your hair – it never works and will be uneven. I am talking from personal experience and yes, it was a botch job.

95. Ghetto Chic
I am not ashamed to say that I shop in economy clothing stores. As a performance artist, I always need to look chic on stage. However, until I become a millionaire, you will find me purchasing cost-effective clothes and accessories. Since losing weight, most of my clothes do not fit and have become shapeless and loose. In this instance, I speak to my stylist Tanya who advised me to become best friends with a sewing needle, belt and to mix and match my clothes.

96. Smart Works
This is a fantastic charity that supports women in London who have been long-term unemployed. The aim is to increase women's confidence by dressing

100 Ways To Save Money

them smartly when attending interviews. Being the curvaceous lady that I am, I was concerned that they would not have my size, however I was happily proven wrong. Smart Works helps by supplying women with a suit, shoes and basic cosmetics. I have used this service and was extremely grateful for the opportunity to feel good in my clothes and, yes, I landed my dream job at the London Bubble Theatre Company. A huge thank you goes out to Delyth Evans and her wonderful team. You can only attend Smart Works based on a referral. For more information, visit: www.smartworks.org.uk.

97. Take Centre Stage
Having a solid background in theatre means that I get a variety of special deals on opening nights and for preview shows. The offers I like the best are paying one-third off the recommended retail price ticket. I have seen productions like 'The Lion King' (Lyceum Theatre) and 'Fela' (National Theatre). I introduced my two sisters to a fantastic under-25s scheme so that they now have the opportunity to attend awesome West End theatre shows for free or pay as little as £5. Join Central London theatre mailing lists or give them a call and find out what special offers are available.

98. Love Music, Don't Abuse it
I am and always will be a music lover as I spend my money frequently on new music. Music lovers everywhere can buy online for less, since digital recordings are very cheap. If you cannot afford to purchase new music in this way, then create an online playlist and listen to the music you love for free. Artists will still be paid their royalties through online payments.

100 Ways To Save Money

99. Smoke-Filled Lungs
If you are an average smoker of 20 cigarettes a day, you could save up to **£2,420.60** a year. Think about what you could do with the spare cash; you could have a cruise, buy a car and most importantly, improve your health significantly. The benefits of quitting smoking are:
1. Fresh breath.
2. Improved fertility.
3. Reduced carbon monoxide in the body.
4. Sometime between 2 to 12 weeks after quitting, your circulation will improve, making walking easier.
5. You will reduce the risk of a heart attack.

100. A Free Workout
Since losing 42 pounds in weight, I am always on the lookout for an opportunity to work out in a cost-effective manner. If you are overweight and have a medical weight-related condition, be sure to check out your local doctor's surgery for an exercise-referral scheme in conjunction with your local gym. This is a 12-week programme and you will be offered a discounted rate. Alternatively, if you do not fall into that category, you can take full advantage of the outdoor gyms in some parks. These are free of charge and you can use them 24 hours a day, seven days a week.

101. A Holey Experience
This is an interesting one and may cause controversy. Nevertheless, I will endeavour to keep it real with my readers and use my perspective to liberate their minds. I have a pair of trainers which I adore because they are super comfortable. I have owned them for a decade and wore them so much that they have now got pea-sized holes in the right foot made by my big

toe. Yes, I could have thrown them out when I finally bought a new pair of trainers, however, to tell the truth, I have kept them to remind me of how hard times have been.

Do not be ashamed if your clothes or shoes are worn out and have seen better days. I am sure if you had money you would replace them. I remember walking in the snow in 2009 and wondering why my socks kept feeling wet. Eventually I investigated and, to my dismay, I discovered a gaping hole at the bottom of my left black, fake, leather boot; what was worse was that I had to wait 2 payday months before I could afford a new pair and could only wear them in dry weather. This does not make me a bad person. I simply fell and banged my head on hard times; it is as plain and clear as the daylight.

102. Become a Detective
Become inquisitive. If something smells fishy, determine where that odour is coming from. I told you previously how I got a huge reduction in savings on online rental for my landline phone and broadband bill. However, I was still receiving high bills which I could not understand. Eventually I decided to investigate and to my horror, I was going over my monthly broadband allowance. I shopped around for an unlimited tariff that would be cost-effective for me in the long run because I upload large videos.

The Enlightened Mind Set

100 Ways To Save Money

103. Using What You Have
I remember doing a blog on this subject for 'Let The Healing Begin'; an online television show. The idea behind it was to generate a platform where I would challenge people's perceptions about reaching their goals. Right now there are people, places and things in your life that can help to transcend your future and offer you a fulfilling destiny. I have never seen the righteous forsaken. If you think about it, there are several opportunities right underneath your nose. You may miss them if you are not paying close attention.

Firstly, observe your vocabulary. I do not use the words 'I can't' because it restricts me into thinking that I do not need to try very hard. The words 'I can't' is a shut door that will never help me or you to progress. Try 'I can', which may mean that you need to take on an evening class to learn how to do something rather than depending on someone else.

I know a struggling actor who is aged 60 and who relies on his son to check his emails. Let's face it, what teenager has got the time to check his dad's emails? They would rather be out partying and having fun. What I did was to offer to train the loveable comic actor to realise he had to be self-reliant. I began to teach him how to send, receive and add attachments to emails. Have you heard of that saying; 'if you give a man a fish you feed him for a day, if you give a man a fishing rod you feed him for a lifetime'? When it comes to the words 'I can't', remove it from your mind and focus on positive self-talk.

104. Fight the Spirit of Complacency
The mind is a powerful tool when used correctly. Decide to embrace positive mental thoughts

100 Ways To Save Money

throughout the duration of your day. Life and death truly lives on the tongue. Be the master of your words and use them to speak positive utterances into your day.

Legendary motivational speakers like Les Brown and Anthony Robbins use Neuro Linguistic Programming in their seminars and conferences to change people's resistant, negative thought patterns. These men have made an impact by changing the language they and their clients use and have become extremely successful millionaires.

By frequently soaking yourself with positive statements and affirmations like 'I deserve the best', 'I am worthwhile', or 'money flows to me in abundance', it helps create a positive mind frame. Make sure you say it with power and conviction and it will eventually feel real. Ponder the above affirmations carefully. Always look at your glass as half-full or, better still, overflowing. Beware of some individuals' total lack of concern and disregard for you, stepping out of your comfort zone and making an impact with your gifts; they will hinder your progress in the arena of life. Do not wallow in the mud with negative people. Instead, move away! Call victory into your life and really visualise success living at your doorstep Complacency is a thief of dreams and is not conducive to being proactive. Remember, you deserve the best life has to offer; now chase your dreams.

105. The Entrepreneurial Spirit
Many entrepreneurs are born out of an economic crisis simply because they have to become more creative and resourceful, particularly if they are on the lower scale income bracket. Becoming self-

employed is not for everyone; you have to work long hours for little or no pay to start off with.

However, if your drive is to lead, then this is a worthwhile option to consider. Actively write down your vision and ideas in a notebook and begin a strategy of how you can take your services to the general public. Do not let the credit crunch paralyse your dreams.

106. Learn How to Use the Word 'NO' Effectively

A strong 'No' is better than a weak 'Yes'. Life's commitments can lead us to over-extend ourselves when helping out loved ones. If you agree to a birthday meal that you cannot afford, then at the heart of the matter you are cheating yourself and increasing your debt. Be honest if you cannot afford a night out: say 'no'. If someone offers to pay for you and you will pay them back, think carefully about your response. Ask the following questions:

* When can I pay them back?
* Can I afford to pay them back?
* Will this person manipulate me if I fail to pay them back early?

This should help you make a wise choice. The word 'no' creates a boundary which people may not like. Remember, it is your budget that will ultimately suffer, not theirs.

107. The Wise Snake

If you are surrounded by a bunch of critical, negative people hanging around your ankles, how do you think they will affect your mental state? Have you ever been on the phone with a friend who drains your energy while they spew their poison into your ears? Their glass is always half-empty and they have a transparent, destructive veil that covers their entire aura. You know the type of person I mean. They walk into a room with a miserable disposition and expect everyone to pander to their needs of what is wrong.

Be like the wise snake that sheds its skin twice per annum; give draining people a gentle nudge out of your life. My next suggestion is to move to the nearest exit extremely quickly. It is diabolical to tolerate excessive negativity, especially if you are not a professional therapist. Be around people who will help you grow and can add value to your life, not deplete it. Today, start shedding those negative people; you will feel better for it and at least your load will not be as heavy to carry.

108. Stop Robbing Peter to Pay Paul Because They Are All Broke

If you recognise that you have a poverty consciousness and also negative thought patterns, your attitude needs changing. When you become aware of this, it is your duty to know, do and act better. One's self-esteem can take an incredible whack if you are constantly focusing on how to move money around. Instead, look at inventive ways of how you can generate an additional income. I hope these words are soaking in and marinating.

109. Remember the Word I.N.S.P.I.R.E!

My business partner and I co-host a popular event called 'I.N.S.P.I.R.E' which is a monthly Showcase and Open Mic night in the heart of the West End (Piccadilly Circus, London). This event gives a welcoming platform to aspiring musicians, singers, dancers and poets. I.N.S.P.I.R.E opens its doors to creative talent and its supporters, as well as housing international artists who have travelled thousands of miles to grace our stage and share their gifts. During the heat of the London riots in 2011, we used our event to encourage the community to engage in a positive manner. Beginners, intermediates and advanced artists shared their art form to express their creativity in an optimistic way. What I would like you to remember is our positive acronym for I.N.S.P.I.R.E:

Inspiring
New
Seasons
Promoting
Internal
Revolutionary
Existence

Use these powerful words to impart courage, strength and motivation in your world. Let this acronym uplift you daily and allow it to impact your being. When you change your thoughts, you can change the quality of your life and you can move mountains.

110. The Power of Purposeful Positive Prayer

If you are a religious person or you believe in a power greater than yourself, then draw closer to your faith or beliefs. Praying is very cathartic. It has been known to uplift the despondent and provide hope for the destitute. I usually pray for family, friends, good health, strength, direction, wisdom and courage. I stay away from self-seeking prayers asking for material possessions; instead, I ask for daily guidance, increased intuition and a vision where there was none. I earnestly seek to fulfil God's purpose for my life through the power of prayer.

100 Ways To Save Money

111. Your Inner Sanctuary
Meditation is a great opportunity to connect to your life-force energy, which is your breath. If this is your first time, find a quiet place, unplug the phone, sit on a chair or lay down on your back. Close your eyes and take a few deep breaths in through your nose and out through your mouth. Clear your mind of all daily activities and become still. Relax by focusing on the furthest sound you can hear. You can also read your favourite biblical scripture or quote before you close your eyes. It is vital to take time out from the corporate rat race and come back to the core of your being. Be sure to listen to that small voice within; it is your intuition speaking.

112. A Free Thinker
Become a free thinker and follow your intuition (that small voice on the inside). Do not take what people say at face value. Think for yourself and see where it takes you. When we become conditioned by what we are told and what we see, we become gullible robots. Today, think outside the box and create a future worth living.

113. The Ceiling
In a regular nine-to-five job, you will only get paid on what your company thinks you are worth. Unless you work in sales, it is very unlikely that you will receive bonuses or become a millionaire working for someone else. Currently, millions of people have been subjected to salary freezes, or in my case a salary decrease for the next 24 months. This is a bummer, especially since inflation feels like it is rising every single day. What can you do? If you have an entrepreneurial spirit and have desired to start your own business, then now is the time to seriously consider taking your destiny into your own hands.

100 Ways To Save Money

114. Karma is a Boomerang
Karma is simply cause and effect: what you put out into the universe is what you get back. Always monitor your intentions behind your actions and deeds. In life, as you tighten your budget, you need to make sure that you have put yourself in a position of good karma. You can do this by treating people with grace and going the extra mile. The natural law is that you will receive the same care and attention you have shown but from a different source.

115. Operating in the Garden of Fear
When operating in the realms of fear, you must dig deep for courage to change your mind-set. Do not allow fear to dominate your life and give you sleepless nights. Being proactive means you put yourself in the driving seat and can navigate yourself out of worry and distressing situations.

116. I Need a Prescription for Addiction
Addictions are expensive habits to have. Recognising that you are chemically addicted is the first step to not only saving money but recognising that you are spiritually evolving and taking care of your health. People become addicted for a variety of reasons which often can stem from unresolved issues in childhood. Usually, the addictive personality type wants to escape their reality in some shape or form by using alcohol, drugs or gambling to medicate their pain and fill the void. If you suspect that you may be addicted, I suggest you please seek help at once. Speak to your doctor or go online and research areas for specific support. Good luck, and remember you are stronger than any addiction.

117. Speak Life into Your Situation
No matter how bad it gets, how cold the wind blows in your life, or how many mountains you have to climb,

100 Ways To Save Money

know that your situation and circumstances can and will eventually change. The tide will turn because nothing lasts forever, even if your perception and outlook is grey and bleak. You may be facing bankruptcy, you may have had your home repossessed, your spouse may have had an affair and left you or you may have 0.02p in your bank account: all of the above do not define who you are or your self-worth. There is an inner strength blu-tacked against your heart and is waiting to be released.

I am speaking to your fighting spirit, and I am asking you to play the tape of your life forward. Think about your family, friends and work colleagues who will experience the grief if you selfishly take your own life. We are here on this planet to experience the good, the bad and the ugly, the twists and swings via this rollercoaster called life. Nothing can be so bad that it cannot be mended or healed.

Talk, get those toxic emotions out of your system, seek professional help or see a counsellor and communicate your needs, desires and wants. Yes, at the depressed points in my life when the financial pressure was at its peak, I admit contemplating taking my own precious life because the spirit of suicide was hounding me. You know what stopped me? I knew that my work here on earth was not completed and I would be robbing so many people from feeling empowered if I selfishly chose to visit a premature grave.

If you think no one cares, you are seriously mistaken. I care; I may not know you directly or we may not have even met in person. Instead, I took the time and faced the loneliness within to write about how you can improve your life by making savvy decisions right now

100 Ways To Save Money

that will empower you. The power is in your hands and if you choose not to use it, which is again your choice, be accountable for the decisions you make.

I believe in your ability to continue to make a positive contribution to your life. My wish for you during this turbulent financial climate is that, you find yourself, like millions of other people, becoming resilient and tapping into your reserve. You have much more to give to the world. Be encouraged and travel well, earthlings, until we meet again.

100 Ways To Save Money

Everyone has a Gift to Share

100 Ways To Save Money

We have all come to earth bearing gifts and talents. Once you discover what your purpose is, life truly opens up in ways that are unimaginable. You will experience things you have never dreamt possible and deep inside, you will feel at peace because you have followed your calling.

I am a creative person and find it a pleasure to tap into my gifts. I asked my dad on Father's Day, 'Were you and my mum singing when you made me?' He laughed. I was serious, because when I hear the drum kick in the music or rhythmic samples used, I normally recognise it instantly. To create is my calling and passion of which I function in daily.

Now it is over to you, I want you to think about what gives you joy in your day to day life. Is it:

- Academia
- Gardening
- Helping people
- Travelling
- Accounting
- Baking
- Listening
- Medicine
- Offering advice

What floats your ship and makes you tingle all over with uncontrollable happiness? What is that hobby that you would love to do for free? It is a known fact that people who follow their passion live longer. Do not use the excuses of 'I am too old, too fat, too black, too young, too scared' to stop you moving forward into your destiny. I do not want to hear it; excuses are for those who desire to remain a victim of their circumstances. This book is about unearthing

100 Ways To Save Money

the diamond in the rough. We need to polish your mind, body and spirit for the world to see the best of you.

Sit down in a quiet place, use the study notes in the back of this book and respond to the following questions:

* What do I enjoy doing?
* What work would I do for free?
* If I could have my dream job, what would it be?
* If money was not an object, what will I be doing?
* What course would I have to study to achieve my passion?

Read back your answers and choose one area to work on vigorously. For example, if you enjoy crunching numbers, make it your goal to develop skills in this area. Use the chart on the next page to map out the next 12 months of how you will develop your knowledge in mathematics. Remember, when you write goals down and plan, your ideas become solidified.

No one can give what you have to offer; you are an original masterpiece. Come into alignment with the greatness that is dormant within you and shine bright like the stars in the sky.

12 Month Hobby Development Plan

January	February	March
April	May	June
July	August	September
October	November	December

Credit Crunch Blues – True Tales of Woe

100 Ways To Save Money

The following are real stories of people I know, who learnt to survive by any means necessary.

It is Getting Hot in Here
I travel frequently to Birmingham to record music and see my second musical family. I have one particular friend who is a sickle-cell suffer, which is made worse by the cold weather. I remember one winter I was in his home and the heater broke down in the kitchen. He had no netting or curtains at the windows so the draught was coming in. He used his quick-witted initiative and went to his four-ring hob cooker and turned it on to keep warm and cooked dinner. Hard times happen every day; it is what it is!

Get on Your Bike
My middle sister Lydia must have been around me way too long because she understands the pressure of the times. During 2010 Christmas, Lydia had a severe throat infection. On Christmas day at 1am when all the public transport stopped running in London, she could not stand the pain any longer and wanted to go to the hospital. Taxi fares at this time of year are double and they quoted her £25 for a 10-minute journey. Lydia, being a student, immediately thought of her bank balance and opted to pay £1 to hire a London Mayor bike and saved over £20 in taxi charges. Well done, sis.

A Tale of Two Soaps
I remember a family member had to use bubble bath once to wash up her dishes. Hey, do not laugh, it is what it is: a real story. Extreme but true.

Lights, Camera, Action
Ten years ago, camera phones were not as visible as they are now. As a teenager, to purchase a digital

camera was practically unheard of. I remember working with a talented singer and poet who urgently needed her image for a flyer. Using her brain, she decided to get four passport-sized photos done in a photo booth. Then she proceeded to get someone to scan her pictures online and she used this image for a year. It got her plenty of gigs and her objective to make more money was met. Be creative and think outside the parameters of your mind.

Orange Peel
I am really surprised at how inventive restaurants can be. I remember using the bathroom and smelling a warm scent of oranges in the air. Tucked away in the corner was a box of orange peel left over from customers' juice drinks. I thought it was quite clever.

A Heavy Load
A very good editor friend of mine narrated how she once ran out of washing powder to clean her clothes. She is a mother of two and needed to make sure her children's clothes were clean for school. Not having the money to buy washing powder, she decided to use washing-up liquid. Unconventional yes, however, in her words she said, 'The washing up liquid cleaned my clothes better than the washing powder.'

Hit the Road, Jack
I have a friend who is a self-employed electrician who would regularly get into disputes with his father whilst living under his dad's roof. One day, his father bluffed once too many times and said, 'Son, there is the door, use it!' For the next six months the electrician would sleep in his van with his tools, while saving for a deposit for his new home, as he thought renting would be a waste of his money. He prided himself on

having no overheads and free membership to the gym.

Every morning, he would get ready for work and go to the gym to get a shower and brush his teeth. He would stop at the cafe for breakfast and in the evening stop by his friend's home for dinner. His story is compelling and demonstrates grit and utter determination. The electrician now owns his own flat which his father now lives in. In some occasion, his father also works for him; the world is a funny place to be in.

100 Ways To Save Money

A Quick Start Guide to Financial Ordering and Basic Budgeting

100 Ways To Save Money

Keep a Regular Budget
I am not the best mathematical genius in the world, however, I have learnt to complete a monthly budget. I currently use an Excel spreadsheet that adds up the sum total of my expenditure. It is really useful. You have to be disciplined in the area of budgeting and be willing to learn. At the end of this chapter, you will find a basic budgeting sheet to get you on the road to money efficiency. If you prefer, you can search online for a digital budget spreadsheet.

Monster Debt
Being a relative of an ostrich and burying your head in the sand will not help improve your debt situation. Face up to your monster debt and be brave. List all of the debts you owe, for example:
> Loans
> Credit cards
> Rent arrears
> Car repayment
> Hire purchase goods

Remember, your priority debts such as rent arrears, council tax, electricity and gas will need to be paid off first. There are some hardship funds you can apply to for help with paying your energy fuel bills. If your budget is extremely tight, you can offer to pay your remaining creditors a token payment of £1 until your financial situation improves. If you do go to court, the Judge will see that you are making an effort by attempting to pay. As long as you keep the communication lines open with these companies that you owe money, they will usually understand your situation.

Emergency Fund
It is vital to create an emergency fund, because

100 Ways To Save Money

the rollercoaster of life will always show up for you. Spending your last penny is a dangerous ground and places you in an unstable frame of mind. Try putting away £5 each week; after a year you will have £260 in your emergency fund. Everyone, including you, needs a buffer and a soft place to land when unexpected emergencies arrive at your doorstep.

You've Got Mail
Open your mail and respond to your creditors. There was a point in my life when I would get indigestion just by hearing the dreaded sound of the post dropping through my letterbox. Seeing my huge pile of mail gave me the jitters and made me feel physically ill. I became so paranoid that just by looking at the back of my letters, I would recognise my bills and what company they came from. When unemployed, I fell into complete denial and refused to open my letters I really could not cope anymore. Ignoring the bills only caused me anxiety and sleepless nights. I felt better when I found the courage to be proactive and to open my letters and respond.

Being Bullied
If you have a passive personality, you can be easily intimidated by the numerous calls from debt collectors. If you are too frightened to speak with them, I suggest you communicate with them via letter or email. This way you can be in control of what you can offer, and not be pressured into paying what you cannot afford.

Educate Yourself
Go to your local library and read up on finances and budgeting. It is the only way you can improve your financial situation. Make use of the helpful links at the

100 Ways To Save Money

back of the book as a starting point. Make sure you are not a victim of the credit crunch and, instead, be a conqueror. Good luck, and remember, do not allow fear to dominate your financial world. Become familiar with basic budgeting figures and be ruthless about sticking to them. Ultimately, it will be for your own benefit and peace of mind.

The following is a basic beginner's budgeting plan which can be amended to suit your individual budget. Make sure you make photocopies of them and use them on a weekly or monthly basis.

100 Ways To Save Money

Monthly Budget Plan

Classification	Monthly Budget Amount (expected)	Monthly Tangible Amount (actual)
INCOME:		
Wages		
Miscellaneous		
INCOME SUBTOTAL		
EXPENSES		
Rent/mortgage		
Gas/Electricity		
TV License		
Council Tax		
Travel		
Car/petrol/tax		
Savings		
Landline phone		
Broadband		
Mobile phone		
Groceries		
Gym		
Spending money		
Clothing		
Child care		
Insurance		
EXPENSES SUBTOTAL		
NET INCOME (Income minus expenses)		

Moving on After the Recession

100 Ways To Save Money

The Story of Money

100 Ways To Save Money

Imagine for a moment, that we had no money, no credit cards, no debit cards and no coins. Visualise an entire world without these things and without anything that was the equivalent. In the world I am describing, if you could not make or grow something yourself, you would hope that you could trade labour, or whatever it was you could produce for that which you wished to obtain.

This was the weakness of the barter system, the value of what you had varied by the person you were trading with. If I desired to own chickens and all you had was wheat, if I did not know someone who specifically wanted wheat then I had no reason at all to trade with you. Your wheat was useless to me if my stores were already overflowing.

If you were particularly lucky, I might know someone who was looking for wheat who would provide something that could, in turn, be able to be traded for the chickens I so desire. As you can tell, this was far from an optimal system, and could lead to some people taking chances, accepting things they did not need in the hope that that they would be able to trade it for something they actually desired.

Make no mistake though, there were strengths to the system as well. If someone particularly desired a resource you had, then that desire is what sets the value of what you have. Michael may want and need a large amount of wheat and only be able to trade you eggs for it. Now, eggs are valuable, used in many types of food. However, they are not something you particularly need. This may result in Michael either not being able to purchase your wheat from you or it may cost him a lot more eggs than it would on another day. If however, Michael had leather to trade, and

100 Ways To Save Money

you particularly desired leather, then that leather would be worth more than wheat to you. Michael, who is the cattle farmer, has the advantage, because he owns an abundance of leather to trade. Every item exchange had a different value to each person you traded with.

This was the way things were since the moment humans started trading items; however, 2,000 years before the birth of Christ, in the ancient land of Mesopotamia, a problem had developed. In the city of Sumeria, there were those of such wealth, possessing such copious amounts of resources and had the ability to trade goods in large volumes, which meant that what they owned could no longer be easily transported to trade with those who desired to receive it. It was simply unrealistic to expect even the lavish and expansive markets of this ancient city to hold all that the traders, especially those who traded in crops, could and in fact needed to get into circulation.

The solution they came to was fairly simple; one would put their grain and crops into the granaries to be found in and around their city and get a receipt for the amount stored there. They would then take these receipts to market and trade that receipt for what they needed from others, who in most cases would then go with the receipt to the granary to extract that which they were due.

This system was far from perfect but it was in fact, the first form of currency to ever exist. It was still mostly barter method, as one could only buy from those who had a desire or a need to possess what was in your granaries. If the person you were buying from did not want wheat, the wheat in your granary became of no value to the buyer, however at least

100 Ways To Save Money

you had not hauled all that wheat to market for the privilege of finding that out.

Within the next 500 years, this area started using metal as a form of currency and it was at that moment when the face of commerce and trade began to change in some very impressive ways. Currency represented something far more fluid than receipts. Currency could purchase anything, provided you had enough of it, as it represented a 'value' rather than an 'amount of a particular commodity'. Additionally, it could be stored indefinitely, as currency was almost always something which did not rot or decay and was much lighter in most cases, than the value which it represented. In this particular example, I am going to stick with metal as the main form of currency.

It was silver that was the first metal currency: small coins measured and weighed according to precise guidelines to maintain a consistent value. These were traditionally marked with an image of some form, which served two purposes. One was to edify the ruler during the time the coins were created, directly associating the ruler of a time with the wealth of his country. The other reason was to create a visible marker which would indicate if any kind of fakery was going on. A common practice of the time was to 'shave' the outside of coins, taking a bit of metal from them and gathering it together to forge a new counterfeit coin or just to sell the melted-down metal. At first, this solved many of the problems of transporting wealth However, with the wealthy and those skilled at keeping the coins; they eventually found that they had obtained too many coins which were unreasonable to carry around with them daily. This created a demand for two things, one of which called back to the original form of currency and the other resulting in an institution we are very familiar with today. Banks had been around for a while in some forms which would be familiar to those of us today; however, decidedly not the same thing.

You see, they were private institutions, not federal or run by the government in any way. The banks served the purpose of storing your wealth, providing you got a certified note indicating how much wealth you actually possessed and in certain circumstances, could even be convinced to put forth loans. Two of the most powerful and well-known of these institutions were the Medici of Italy and the Fuggers of Germany. The process was relatively simple; you made a deposit at one branch of this banking organisation and would receive a bank note for your trouble. This note was far easier to transport over the vast miles between your point of departure and your destination than the large amounts of currency a trader might just need to travel.

You would of course be charged a fee when you withdrew your money at the new location. However, it would not be your money, not the money you left with them that it is. Instead, you would be withdrawing an amount of money equal to somewhat less than your deposit (to cover the fee), from an equal or greater amount that had been deposited by some other person or persons. The system expanded all over Europe from this point forward, making trade flow easier than ever, and because of this, Europe for the time flourished with commerce and trade.

There were many innovations and changes from this point on; the foundations of banking remain much the same, different only in how they adapt to the modern age. Medici and Fugger banks were not precisely

100 Ways To Save Money

'protected', so it was possible that a particular bank could be robbed during wartime or just by enterprising criminals, and there was nothing to guarantee that you would be able to get your money back. That did not come about until federal governments started insuring financial institutions in the interest of providing some form of security for those people who stored their money there.

One of the most important innovations to come about for those of us depositing our money was the concept of interest. Interest is one of the most basic ways to help turn your money from a little bit into a lot more. However, most people do not understand why interest even exists; they merely accept that it does and try and get the best interest rates on the market.

When a bank stores your money, you can almost guarantee that the money is in turn being used to back loans for cars, houses, businesses and even personal signature loans. The bank is being paid a percentage on those loans and you in turn are being paid a percentage for permitting the bank to utilise your money. The truth of the matter is that percentage is actually there to encourage you to leave your money in the bank rather than taking it out and spending it. If the money is not in the bank, the bank does not have money to draw on for loans.

This is why things like <u>Certificates of Deposit</u> and such have higher interest rates, however they come with a fee if you withdraw them before they are 'mature'. You are promising when you purchase one of these to leave your money in the bank for a certain amount of time. The higher interest rate is a 'reward' or thank you from the bank for them being able to invest in that money being there for a certain amount of time.

100 Ways To Save Money

The fee for withdrawing early is of course a penalty for violating that promise. The world of banking is a vast and complex place, and what we have touched on above is only the tip of the iceberg when it comes to ways to save your money and how the entire banking system works, especially as banks are no longer a solid solution to build on.

How to Prevent Financial Chaos
Sometimes, it seems as if our debt takes on a mind of its own. At the beginning of the month, we set out a budget with the best of intentions and start off earnestly trying to follow it. Money seems to leak out through mysterious holes as we partake in minor indulgences that lead up to a deluge of debt as the month creeps on. We keep paying on our credit cards, yet the balance never seems to go down, and our thoughts of one day seeing ourselves with a positive balance in the account just seem to constantly fades as time goes on.

What is it that causes this? Why does the slide into financial ruin seem unavoidable, steady, and unrelenting? In many cases it is because we simply do not understand the nature of our own financial situation and what steps we can take to help work our way out of our predicament. The never-ending ring of the phone seems to herald the march of debt-collectors at our doors.

The first step is a simple one, though it seems to be the hardest action for a lot of people recently. Saving just a small portion of your income each month in a separate account that you do not touch is a wonderful way of setting up a nest egg; however, there are other reasons as well. If you make just £1,500 a month after taxes, saving 10% of your income each

100 Ways To Save Money

month would put £150 aside, or £1,800 a year. This may seem a small amount, however, it can be very important in the event of an emergency or when planning to take care of other debts.

Your bills are particularly important. Many companies charge late fees if they are not paid on time, and even if it is just £25 a month worth of charges, that adds up £300 a year, or $1/6^{th}$ of the amount you are trying to save each month in the above example. Be sure to check your various bills and utilities, and if one must be paid late, pay it to the one with the smallest late fee - every little bit helps!

Paying off your debts quickly is an important part of making your current situation manageable. We are going to use a credit card as an example of why this is important. Let us assume that you have a credit card with a 12% interest rate per annum and a £2,000 balance. Every month, that 12% interest rate is going to result in your balance going up by £20, if you are paying the minimum payment of interest, which means that after that first payment you will be looking at a balance of £19.60. That 12% interest will charge you £19.60 on the next bill for interest.

If you make another £60 payment, the new balance will be £1,920.40. As you can see, at this rate it will take you forever to pay off this debt. Making larger payments will bring down your bill further and in turn, will reduce the amount of interest you are paying. If you have been saving 10% of your income monthly in the example mentioned previously, then this will allow you to make what is called 'balloon payments'. These are larger payments that drive down your overall expenses quicker and immediately reduce how much you will be paying in interest with each subsequent cycle.

There are many financial commitments that carry with them this kind of ever-increasing debt; mortgages, car payments, any form of loans of any kind. Paying larger payments to them, or saving to make occasional balloon payments, will help you conquer these debts and end up owing less in the long run. Remember, managing your debt and avoiding late fees while saving for the future will help reduce the financial chaos that tries to ruin most of our lives.

100 Ways To Save Money

A to Z Guide on How to Become Self-Employed

100 Ways To Save Money

Introduction

It is important not to be reliant on the state for long-term benefits. I do not believe in the 9-to-5 ethos and waiting to receive a state pension with a gold clock at the age of 65. It would not surprise me if the government increase retirement age to 70 by the time I am ready to retire. I am all about you creating your own income streams with the talents and resources that you currently have. At the very least I would want you to work in a job where YOU get job satisfaction on a daily basis. What is the point in waking up every morning feeling depressed about going into work or being unemployed. You need to find the strength within you to make better choices for your career.

100 Ways To Save Money book is my contribution to the world; it is my gift to you. My aim is to help you get out of the rut which is the recession. If you have ever considered being self-employed, this A to Z guide will give you a great basic overview on what is needed to get you started. Being your own boss sounds great, however let me tell you it is not an easy road, and you will indeed have to roll with the punches and roll with the kicks as well as working long hours.

A. Do What You Enjoy

The key to life I believe is making sure that you are functioning in your passion. You were born with a unique blueprint calling on your life and it is your duty to pursue your purpose in its entirety. When you find a job you enjoy and love, you will never have to work another day in your life. Write down three hobbies that you will try over the next six months to help you

100 Ways To Save Money

expand your horizon. There is nothing like bouncing out of bed when that alarm clock buzzes, and you are fresh-eyed and waiting to start a new day. You deserve the best life has to offer. We spend over half of our lives at work; why not make it fun along the way.

B. Take What You Do in Business Seriously

When starting a new business or creating a passive income, take your services seriously. The reason why I say this is, because your customers buy into what you say as the main representation of your products and services. Keeping on track with emails and phone calls are key, and shows you are serious about your brand and making a great first impression. Many people describe their services as suitable for everyone which is incorrect. You cannot have a product or service that everyone would like or love. This shows your green leaf mind-set; what you need to think about is your consumer research. Once this is done, you can corner a niche market to sell your products and services too. For example, if you are a fashion designer selling maternity wear, it is no good saying this is an ideal outfit for schoolgirls. You will never make any money. We have the Internet at our fingertips and we can certainly investigate all which is not clear in business. By doing research on your start-up business, you are taking what you do seriously and are ready for the long haul of the business world.

C. Meticulous Planning
I am meticulous when it comes to planning. Whether it is a family member's birthday party or planning an event in the West End, I make sure that I plan everything to the finest detail. To begin with, I always write down my ideas, I plan the guest list and if it is a

show, I work out the timings and a schedule for when the artists are due on stage. I create a marketing strategy of how we will contact our target audience and media promotions.

Normally, this is done via emails, texts and social media. When you have a plan, your goals become solidified and you are able to tick off your check list of what is completed as you go along. Do not be too hard on yourself if you do not achieve your targets, everything is adjustable. If you fail to plan, then you plan to fail. You have to develop strategies that will assist you on the ladder of success. It is vital to have and create a five-year projection plan for your business. This is a must, so you have tangible goals to work towards and a destination to reach.

D. Manage Your Money Wisely

The majority of millionaires I know are very frugal with their money and do not spend it unless it is absolutely necessary. In fact, they like to spend other people's money through investments and sponsorships. Take a lesson out of their book and begin to model those who are living, breathing, walking, and talking success. Small-business owners cannot waste time, money and energy on promotional activities aimed at building awareness solely through long-term repeated exposure. If they do, chances are they will go bust long before their business really takes off. There are lots of free courses to help manage your company's money better; all you have to do is to be open to finding out new information and learning. Once you can do basic book-keeping in business, your business will soar. Excel and Sage are excellent packages to work with. My mentor trained me on Excel and it helps me with my book-keeping.

100 Ways To Save Money

E. Ask For What You Want

You must by any means necessary be bold in business. If you do not ask for what you want, you will not get it. The worst that can happen is that you will be refused with a 'No'; if you can push past a 'No' until you get a 'Yes', then that is progressive thinking. Only the strong survive in this dog-eat-dog professional world. Believe in yourself, believe in your brand, believe in your service and believe in your product.

If your strength is not in the area of selling, you need to find an expert who you can outsource the work to, or at the very least, learn how to sell. There are lots of free resources on YouTube on this topic; I suggest you look up Motivational Speaker, Anthony Robbins. Watching Anthony has given me an injection of strength when I was flagging. He has great techniques to improve your life in the area of selling and personal development. You must constantly make an attempt to improve knowledge in your weak areas of your business; this will help improve on your business acumen. An example of this is: I am dyslexic, yet I have written four books; I have never let my learning difficulty stop me from achieving my career goals.

When I first launched my website www.lyricalhealer.co.uk, this site was based on a template where I could make changes to the calendar or update the adverts. In order to make these changes, I had to learn basic HTML codes. I am no computer whizz by any means, however, I taught myself enough to become self-efficient. I asked the website designer to train me up and I was ready to go with a few mistakes along the way. You will always

100 Ways To Save Money

learn and grow through the mistakes in your business; it is a part of your growth. When you have the courage to step up and say 'This is what I require, can you help me?' you are set apart, because what you are doing is being proactive in your approach to business.

When people observe your heart and passion for your company, they will naturally gravitate towards you and offer their services to help you on your journey. It is called following the ebb and flow of your life. Have the courage to open doors that were previously closed and work through them with confidence and vigour. Unlock the magic door of reciprocity and see how you can benefit today.

F. Remember, Be Customer Driven

Without your customers, you have no people to sell your products or services to. In business, you MUST put yourself in your customer's shoes at all time. Never design or create a new product based on what you want, this process is not about you. Please consider how you can provide a quality product or give exceedingly value for service and go beyond the customer expectations. The idea is to make sure that you get repeat orders when upselling your high-end services. Word of mouth is the most powerful form of sales. If you can generate a buzz around your services, this is a great public relation tool. Customers buy from you because of how you make them feel. They will always remember the 'feel good' factor of the great service or products you provide. When starting out, a great way to build is in your immediate network, get the support of family and friends and build from there. If your product is good enough, then word of mouth recommendations will spread like wild fire.

G. Become a Talking Poster

There is nothing wrong with self-promotion as long as you are not obnoxious with it, as it can put potential buyers off. Always promote the benefits of the product and not how great you are at bringing the product to the market quite simply put. Buyers want to know what is in it for them. Find out what the buyers' needs are and then offer them solutions to their problems by using your product or service. A great tool when it comes to networking is to be an active listener and make sure you reiterate what the person is saying back to you.

Show a genuine interest in what they do, while in your head you are analysing how your services or network can add value to them. Once you understand who you are networking with, you can determine if this person can add value to your brand. Find out what your potential clients needs are first, then proceed with your best 60 second elevator pitch. Be clear on what your business does, what you do and the services or products you provide; make sure when you speak that you are filled with confidence while making good eye contact. If you are well-known for your positive contribution within your sector, normally, people will come to you and ask about your services or how the product is selling. This demonstrates that you are building a great reputation among your peers.

H. Project a Positive Business Image

Image is everything and how you present yourself in the world of business will determine your future income streams. It is vital that when you step into a room, your clothes announce you. People make up their mind about you in the first three seconds of meeting you. This includes your non-verbal cues. I am a tomboy at heart, I love to wear comfortable clothes and have no interest in the slightest being a girly-girl. My personal stylist, Tanya, tells me off about this all the time and often reminds me that I need to present the correct image that matches my brand. She even advises me on the clothes that do not suit my body shape, for example, like leggings; she says they are 'too casual and highlight cellulite'.

I am more than happy to wear jogging bottoms and a t-shirt. However, in the corporate world in which I have now become accustomed to, this is unacceptable. Dressing smart is totally out of my comfort zone; I am naturally creative at heart and crave bright colours. Therefore, I have learnt that in order to bring my 'A game', I have had to look past that and purchase some business suits that are not trouser-based. Once you have a professional look, corporates and the business world will take you more seriously. As a result you can secure that huge contract that you have been dreaming of.

I. What Are Your Customer's Needs?

A common mistake that start-up businesses make is not identifying their customer's needs. This is quite instrumental when it comes to marketing and advertising your services to them. You need to know where they are located and you cannot do that with

100 Ways To Save Money

guesswork. You have to be precise and think of the following:

1. How do they buy products?
2. What are their spending habits?
3. Where do they eat?
4. Are they single or married?
5. What is their age?
6. What is their ethnicity?
7. How much disposable income do they earn?
8. What is their demographic?
9. What magazines or newspapers do they read?
10. What television shows do they watch?

The above are a few sample questions to get you started; please be aware this is a sample and there are many more.

You then need to build a profile of each customer, and create a strategy of how to approach them in order to capture your attention with your services and products. You may require a professional service to assist you with this. Make sure you build a strong fan base and continue to be consistent in updating your customers with news and services that they may be interested in. Mailchimp and Constant Contact are great ways to create newsletter contact and keep in with your clients. Once you have researched your niche market, it will be easier to sell directly to them.

J. Level the Playing Field with Technology

In this new and exciting millennium, anyone can be a rapper, singer or book author. The landing of social media in our front rooms and on our phones wherever we go means we can have our own identity or office at our fingertips. For example, if you use a YouTube channel effectively, you have your own television show, which means you have the potential of broadcasting into the homes of millions worldwide especially if your video becomes viral. Straight away, you have free marketing and a PR tool when you tell your story, and if it is of interest to the general public, you will be a huge hit with millions of views.

Through my network, I have been able to create a database with thousands of emails; communication is my gift and I am very comfortable speaking to strangers. It does not intimidate me to be in a room full of strangers as I thrive on standing on my own. Sometimes in life, you have got to know, as a leader, that you will have to walk alone in your vision; there are some places your family or friends cannot go. If you are sitting down saying 'I do not even know how to turn a laptop on', do not make that as an excuse as to why you failed in business. You can employ someone who is computer literate in your business to train you and help with the day to day running. However, you will never fully understand their role in your business and frankly, that is not a good sign. Enrol in being part of the solution; take a night class and learn to improve your information technology skills. When you level the playing field, you have greater opportunities to play with the 'big wigs'. Be sure to fully utilise your social media networks as this will benefit your business.

K. Build a Top-Notch Business Team

Have you ever heard of that saying 'You are known by the company you keep'? Transfer this to your business. You have to create a team around you that is waterproof and trusted; currently, I have a small core team of ten which consists of the following:

100 Ways To Save Money

- Manager
- Personal Manager
- Project Manager
- 8 Workshop Facilitator's
- Administrator
- Personal Stylist
- Photographer
- Two Song Writers
- Two Volunteers

The rest of the roles like Graphic Designer, Marketing Assistant and book printing, I outsource internationally. You have to learn the art of delegation and learn to rely on your team to play their part. I once worked for a very successful businessman, but he was a nightmare to work for because he would not let go of the reigns and let me lead on the area of my expertise. Needless to say, I left after six months of this nonsense because as a staff member, I did not have time to deal with his control and ego issues.

Becoming you own boss is rewarding, but remember you will have countless sleepless nights and will be spending a lot of energy in putting the business together and getting it off the ground. You must work with people you trust and who are reliable, and remember, ALWAYS get at least two references from previous employers for potential employees.

L. Become Known as an Expert in Your Field

If your specialist area is on 'bee keeping,' you must stand out against your competitors. For example, your name must come up first in the search engine. If it does not, you need to find a person that specialises in Search Engine Optimisation (SEO) and make sure they move your name up to the top ranking, or at the very least the top three results of 'bee keeping'. This will be a great way to drive more traffic to your business and sell your goods and services. When you are the guru of your topic matter, clients will fall over themselves to purchase your services and find out more about what you have to say. Imagine the global opportunity that will arise if thousands of people know what you do and how to access your service.

M. Create a Competitive Edge

There must be a reason why a customer comes to you to purchase and buy your services or products. What can you provide that your competitors cannot offer? Think about the gaps in your industry and how you can provide solutions. Do consider partnerships with organisations/individuals that have more extensive knowledge than you and can add value to your business. You need to research other companies similar to your field and improve upon what they do. This is not cheating, this is simply making sure you and your brand stands out. Knowledge is the key to success and in order to know where you are going, you have to know where you are coming from. My competitive edge is this book you are reading. No other organisation can duplicate this or teach classes based on the text in this book without a licence and written permission from me. As the author, I assert my copyright because this is my intellectual property. When I teach my Proactive Employment Workshops this book is the resource I use. This book is my unique selling point and competitive edge in the field of employability.

N. Invest in Yourself

If you own a car, you must be aware in order for you

100 Ways To Save Money

to maintain the smooth running of it on the road, you will need to have the following:

- MOT
- Services
- Tyre pressure checked
- Insurance
- Car wash cleaning bills
- Petrol costs
- Regular oil changes

Without these things, your car simply will not work. It is a necessity to make sure you invest in your personal development. If you are not centred and focused, how can you run a business? Spend at least one or two days a month on strategic planning for your business, figure out what areas you need to develop in and take proactive steps to making sure you cover your bases in the area of improvement. You must always make sure that you get a complete balance of work, play and rest. Burn out is unpleasant, unattractive and causes exhaustion. You can listen to motivational speakers on the Internet and learn how they stay on track when they feel like giving up. There are countless free online courses or seminars you can listen to or attend. Throughout my personal development sessions, I have been able to work on:

- How to be a confident speaker
- How to win and make friends
- How to influence people
- The power of positive thinking

I simply looked at the weak areas in which I want to develop and improve, then I read books, brought CDs and spoke to professionals in that field. Having these additional skills equips me in handling networking opportunities.

O. Be Accessible to the Public

Pay attention to your fans, supporters and customers, because they are the ones who will put you in a position of having a passive income. Always show appreciation to your network and try your best to keep the links of personal contacts, especially in the world of social media. Yes, you must consider your exclusivity as it makes your brand more appealing. However, never forget your personal touch and even if you are super busy, you can go online and use Hoot Suite to time your daily social media updates. When your customers feel like they can access you, it gives them a sense of personal touch. I recommend spreading the good news about your company on Twitter, Facebook and LinkedIn, because they are the main key areas.

P. Build a Rock Solid Reputation

Be known in your business circles for having a good reputation. Be on time and arrive 15 minutes early for events you have been booked for. Respond to email communications and phone calls regularly or get your receptionist to make call-backs when you are super busy. Pay your staff on time; make working with you a total pleasure so that staff would like to continue helping you build your business, even if they are volunteering their time.

Q. Sell the Benefits

When you create a great quality product, your network will naturally contribute towards the selling of your product. They will do this by Facebook posts and Twitter feeds. Customers do not want to hear how good you think you are. They want to hear about themselves and how their lives can be improved by the product or service. When someone has the information about how your product or service can improve their lives, it will be easy for them to make an informed choice. For example, if you say 'buy my book because I put a lot of effort into it' versus: 'This book has more than 100 ways to cost-effective living that will help you save money in the area of household, bills, finances and budgeting'; which statement would you prefer?

R. Get Involved

In the beginning of start-up businesses, all hands are going to have to be on deck. Rome was not built in a day, this is for sure; I know more hands make less work. Sometimes in the early stages of business, you may need to cover all departments, especially if you have not got a huge budget to pay yourself. Even if you cannot afford to have full-time staff members in your business, you can set aside some money for a part-time freelance assistant for a few hours per week. When you build your company from the ground up, you will be surprised at how rewarding it can be when you reach the heights of success. Roll up your sleeves and get stuck in.

S. Grab the Headlines

Use press and media to let the world know your business and services exist. Start with local press as they are very good in writing up articles on home-grown talent. Contact local businesses in your borough and see how you can work together;

associating with larger organisations will put your business in a position of power. Once you generate a buzz in your local community, it gives you a great platform to contact the national press who may even pick up your story and contact you if it is catchy. Free publicity is always good. Another great way to spread the message is to use bloggers to write reviews about your products. When potential clients Google you, they will see a strong feed of online articles that will support how much credibility you have.

T. Work Life Balance

You have to learn to be effective in business. This means you need some down time to collect your thoughts, rejuvenate your mind and mentally prepare for the week ahead. Choose one day out of the seven when you can do this. Some entrepreneur fanatics suggest working all the hours God sends or getting up at 3am. I really believe it is a personal choice. Running yourself into the ground is not good when it comes to your holistic health and mental well-being. If you are going to be doing this full-time then you must enjoy it and not stress out. I have only learnt this in 2013 via my Corporate Business Mentor, Lorna Stewart. She taught me that I can achieve more when I take care of myself and get adequate rest.

U. Business Courses

In this day and age of the recession, many corporate businesses have closed, like 'Woolworths' and 'Our Price' who were giants at the height of their boom. Just because you open a business, it does not mean that it will stay open; the failure rates for new business closing are:

100 Ways To Save Money

Year 1	25 %
Year 2	36 %
Year 3	44 %
Year 4	50 %
Year 5	55 %

Statistics from:
http://www.statisticbrain.com/startup-failure-by-industry/

The statistics to me is extremely alarming; business owners are shocked by the workload it takes to continue to stay open in business, especially if they rent or own a premise. If you are a creative person like me, you can find completing funding applications laborious. I had to learn how to develop a strong business acumen and improve in my weak areas. Throughout my eight years in business, I have been on many courses, mostly free, but some I did have to pay for. I have been able to learn key skills like:

- How to network effectively
- How to be an effective book-keeper
- How to spot potential or key opportunities
- How to sell to your target audience
- How to capture customer details

V. Know Your Niche Market

I really dislike it when I hear that a product is for 'everyone' immediately. It creates alarm bells because I understand that the business owner has no clue about reaching the needs of their client base. It is impossible to have a product that serves everyone. I do not like avocado because it is too creamy, rich and nutty. If you present it to me to eat and tell how fabulous it will taste and sprinkle gold dust on it, I still would not eat it. Why? Because I do not like it. However, if you approached me and said I have a wonderful avocado face mask that will make you look ten years younger, then you have got yourself a sale. Never be wrong and strong in business, always have a listening ear and provide a quality service, and more importantly, know who your customers are and how to sell to them.

W. Get Your Legal Matters in Order

In business, you need to decide if you are going to be a Sole Trader, Limited company, Not for Profit Social Enterprise or a registered charity. HMRC provides current and up to date information on the best options for you. Please be aware that by taking on one of these entities, it means you will have legal responsibilities like:

1. Paying your tax on time.
2. Keeping receipts, invoices and paperwork.
3. Paying National Insurance contributions.
4. Adhere to HMRC company rules and policies.

Know what you are signing up for. I hear so many people talking unnecessarily; they have this elaborate idea for business but no strategy of how they will get there. Do not get caught out, prepare yourself with the knowledge and the facts and with a little effort, you can go very far. For further details please visit: www.hmrc.gov.uk.

100 Ways To Save Money

X. The Launch

Once your company is set up and ready to trade, you will need to have a launch and invite your target audience to attend. Offer them a discount that is a redeemable voucher in the next 30 days of the launch if they buy on the night. Try and get a celebrity, local mayor or MP to attend and invite the press. Your press release must go out two weeks before the event to newspapers and radio stations. I got trained by a journalist and a PR manager on how to write a good press release, and it has been such a valuable skill to learn.

Y. Conquer the Art of Negotiation

Always remember that mastering the art of negotiation means that your skills are so finely tuned that you can always orchestrate a win-win situation. You have to be hard-nosed in business and know what you are worth. I have heard so many times: 'We do not have money because we are a charity or just starting up'. To be frank, that is not your problem. You obviously can have a charitable side in business to what you do. However, you still have bills to pay. Be open to negotiations; never feel like you are selling yourself short, otherwise you will end up becoming resentful. If the rate offered for your services is too low, then politely decline. Creating a win-win situation means that everyone involved feels they have won.

Z. Get a Business Mentor

Last but by no means least, I suggest you get a business mentor or a business coach to assist you along the road to a successful business. If you are really serious about making a full-time living from what you do, then you have to find someone in business that is currently a success. The benefits of working with a mentor will mean consulting decision-making with them to see if you are on the right track. Telling them what is not working is instrumental because they can offer guidance on how to rectify that situation.

For over a year, I have had a business mentor and life coach, Lola Owolabi, who works with me on a monthly basis to help me excel and be great. If I am honest, sometimes I do not like hearing what she has to say because she is challenging me to move beyond my comfort zone. However ultimately I knew that her feedback was for my overall good. A role of a mentor or coach is to offer suggestions, advice and direction, not instruct you on what to do; it is important you know this.

Ideally, you must work with someone you can trust and make sure you build a great rapport with them. My mentor and life coach gives me monthly tasks and homework to complete and I must get it done or we do not have our session. I never knew the relevance of strategic planning in my business. I kept going like a racehorse and never once sat down to think about where my business was heading in the long term. As a result of working with Lorna and Lola, I have built up my confidence, increased my prices and have begun to move in a wider circle of influence. Ultimately, you are the final decision-maker in your business; however, I highly recommend that you do not move ahead without a business mentor in your corner to whom you can be accountable to.

100 Ways To Save Money

It is vital that you enjoy the business process and be open to learning along the way. When you are faced with the tongue of criticism, listen and thank them politely. Breakdown and analyse what has been said, pick out what is the truth and where you can improve. Try your hardest not to take business matters personally, and grow a thick skin with nerves of steel. As a creative person, I have had to learn that there is no room for emotions in business; I had to learn this the hard way. If you are really serious about making a lasting change in your life and helping others put food on their tables because they work for you, then you need to be focused. If you do decide to walk down the road of owning your own business, do it with a positive attitude and always think of your glass as half full. When challenges arise, think business-based solutions.

There you have it; these are my A to Z basic suggestions to begin your journey on the road to self-employment. It is not an easy road; however, it is worthwhile and rewarding. You will get to meet a variety of interesting people and have the opportunity to achieve extraordinary things when you are aligned with your work and purpose. Read books by successful business owners who have gone before you and learn their success model. I will leave you with my worksheet that I provide in my Proactive Employment Workshops. It is a summary of what you have just read. I believe it is good for participants to have something tangible to take away and reflect on after our session is completed.
Good luck on your business journey.

Best wishes,
Winsome Duncan
(The Healer In Me)

100 Ways To Save Money

TOP TEN TIPS ON HOW TO GET EMPLOYED

In order to advance in the world of business, you are required to bring your finest to the table of life. When you leave a room, you want to make sure your potential network remembers you; this means you must excel and be an expert in your field.

1. MAKE A DECISION TO BE GREAT – Today, you need to make a decision to excel in your greatness and make that decision in cement. As of today, tell yourself you will not let any obstacle prohibit your success. Once you have a concrete mind-set, you will attract a world of opportunities.

2. STEP UP YOUR A-GAME – Always be on time as it shows your professionalism. Work on your weak areas and take massive action to improve on them. When someone criticises you or your work, ask yourself: is there any truth in what they say and how can I improve on myself or services?

3. KEEPING UP APPEARANCES – You must look the part, no excuses. When you meet someone for the first time, they make up their mind about you because 90% are non-verbal cues. I am creative by nature, however, when I stepped into the corporate world of business, I had to step outside of my comfort zone and purchase several suits. My presentation in business arena is more pleasing to potential clients.

4. VOLUNTEER YOUR TIME - Securing a job is a full-time job and if you lack skills in your field of expertise, your competitors will win every time. You must gain additional experience by volunteering; this will perfect your skills. Once you have more work experience, you will be able to secure a job.

100 Ways To Save Money

5. RESEARCH YOUR COMPETITORS – This advice is priceless whether you are setting up your own business or looking for a job. You have to find out what others do in their field of expertise and find a way to do it ten times better. Knowledge is power and can never be taken away from you.

6. FREE BUSINESS COURSES – You will gain so many additional skills by searching online for free courses to attend. I have had the benefit of attending Child Protection, Mentoring Level 3, How to Set up Your Business, Build Your Brand and Conflict/Resolutions Techniques training, all for FREE.

7. FAKE IT 'TIL YOU MAKE IT – Take a couple of deep breaths and smile. This is crucial, especially when you are in an interview with senior management or pitching your services to potential buyers. They do not need to know you are nervous; be sure to make direct eye contact without staring and relax.

8. BELIEVE IT AND YOU CAN ACHIEVE IT – Affirmations are short, positive sentences that you repeat to yourself with conviction. Affirmations work best when you say them within the first 20 minutes of waking up in the morning. An example of this is 'I am a confident and successful person in business'.

9. UTILISE YOUR NETWORK – When networking, always find out what the other person does and then figure out how you can be of service to them. You must become an active listener as you can secure future contracts when you know what their needs are and how you can offer them a solution.

10. BECOME A PERSON OF INFLUENCE – Be the head and not the tail. You want people to come to you because of your expertise in your field. A person of influence gets to live exceptional lives and attend events where the elite reside. You deserve a life that is phenomenal and governed by influential people and businesses.

100 Ways To Save Money

Employment Guide: Work Life after Leaving Prison

From
THE STREETS to SCOTLAND YARD
A broken street cycle by Gwenton Sloley   Second Edition

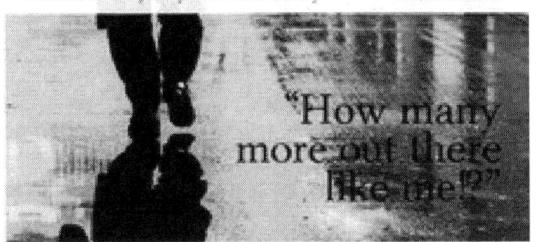

"How many more out there like me?"

100 Ways To Save Money

Introduction
I have a passion for working with disaffected, young people. Frequently, many of their peers and the organisations that work with them give up on them when they are at their lowest; rock bottom. My drive is to serve and offer support where I can help to empower, uplift and inspire those who find themselves in turbulent waters. Having worked with the Metropolitan Police Lambeth Summer Scheme project, Pupil Referral Units and Youth Offending Team, I understand the strong need to educate these individuals to make better choices.

After the riots in 2011, I was invited to deliver a workshop in Wandsworth Prison for Black History Month. I gave a motivational talk about this book and encouraged inmates to live their dreams. Just because they are in prison does not mean that they cannot go and be inspired to do great things after they have served their time. I then finished the workshop with a poetical performance to help uplift and motivate them to excel in life.

When I met Gwenton Sloley, I was stunned by how he had turned his life around in the past nine years since he left prison. He never allowed failure to be an option for him; with an incredible work ethic to match his business acumen, he excelled to the point that he now works with the Scotland Yard Gangs Unit.

In this section of the book, I will let Gwenton's story encourage you to think that no matter what your circumstances have been, you can make a new choice and find several job opportunities if you take proactive action. This is Gwenton Sloley's story.

100 Ways To Save Money

Gwenton Sloley Story
Time rolled by without any warning and I was now seven months into my freedom. I was visiting my parole officer once a week as required. Since the police had not come knocking, I took that as a sign that my behaviour so far had been acceptable and I started to get comfortable with my new routine. I had an excuse before as my step-mum would be hollering at both me and my step-brother, Damion, to get a job or do something constructive with our time.
"You boys have had the same opportunities as everybody else."
"What is the point?" I answered back, "It is not like employers are going to want to employ someone fresh out of jail, besides, I am still on parole."

I would listen to her attentively; promise sincerely that I would get on the job search. It worked all the time. She left the house for work and I nestled back into my bed. For the next few months, I would then tiptoe around her in the house, with the hope she would not question me about career choices or ask how my job search was going. My step-mum gave me good advice, however, if you already have a criminal record and have served your time, you now face a tough challenge securing employment. How do you find a job when you cannot pass a background check? Or how do you explain the three-year gaps since your last job? Everyone needs a source of income and when no one will hire you, it is no wonder ex-offenders return to their former habits and end up back in jail.

Currently, we are in a tough economy with a host of qualified individuals without the burden of a criminal record and being unsuccessful in their job search. It is forcing all unemployed people to seek out resources

100 Ways To Save Money

and become creative in a job search and their career choices. While some ex-offenders may have skills and experience, they have the added hurdle of convincing a potential employer to take a chance that they have left their former life behind and can be trusted to do a job with honesty and integrity without jeopardising the company or its employees.

Finding employment for an ex-offender is difficult; however, it is not impossible. There are resources and strategies to help in the search. The following will help generate ideas for employment.

Start Early

If you are an ex-offender and the end of your sentence is in sight, check to see if your prison has any programmes to help you prepare for release. Utilise comprehensive resources that are available for those preparing for, or recently released.

Some of the major roadblocks to employment for ex-offenders are background checks, bad driving records and suspended drivers licenses. This back to work guide has information on what an inmate can do while still incarcerated to gather the documents needed to restore a driver's licence and obtain a birth certificate and other documents needed to apply for a job.

Some prisons offer classes on how to write a CV and application, explain gaps in employment and answer tough questions that will be presented by the employer. Getting some of these tasks out of the way before release can help keep the momentum going once your sentence is finished.

100 Ways To Save Money

Back To Work Guide for Inmates - Rules for Applications and CVs

To an employer your CV is going to be pretty standard, except for a gap which represents your incarceration. "Convicted Ex-offender" is not a bullet point on your CV; but the truth of your incarceration will most likely be a question on an application or an interview question when selected. The word of the day is 'honesty' when being interviewed.

When you see the question, "Have you ever been convicted of a crime?" you can answer two ways. About 80% of employers do background checks, so you may get lucky if you leave it blank. "No" is a lie and falsification of an application. It is grounds for immediate termination in most companies. If you get fired, you are not only a convicted ex-offender with no job but also have a termination on your job history. "Yes" may stop the process before it begins, however, some employers will appreciate your honesty and give you a chance. In most boroughs, a conviction over seven years ago is not reported and you could answer "No" honestly. Read the question and explanation carefully and answer honestly.

Tough Questions, Gentle Answers

When the subject of your criminal record comes up, there is no need to go into detail. They know the story from the background check. The best thing is admit to making mistakes in the past; however, you have made your amends and have learned a lot and are mentally ready to begin a new life. You have moved on and looking forward to working hard, learning as much as possible and making a positive contribution to the company. Do not look back and always keep your focus on the future.

Ex-Offenders Need Not Apply
There are some jobs that will be off limits. Sex offenders or those convicted of sexual assault may not be able to work at most companies, especially around children or those who are vulnerable and at risk. If you lost your licence or have a lot of driving bans or alcohol-related convictions, jobs that require the use of a company vehicle are unavailable, since the employer's insurance will not cover you. Convictions for theft, embezzlement or credit card fraud are at risk for any position handling money and customer credit card or bank information. Companies are responsible for the safety of their employees and customers at all times. A company can be found negligent and liable for damages for an employee's actions if an employer disregarded warning signs and hired an employee with this history.

Start Your Own Business
This is one of the best options for ex-offenders because you never have to go through a background check and never have to worry about being fired. The best businesses are low cost start-ups. Look for something you can do at home on your computer or services where people want to pay you to come to them. This avoids renting a storefront or office. Here are my examples:

Windshield repair
 People pay you to come to their house and repair dings in their windshield. You can purchase a kit, practice on windshields in a scrap yard until you are

100 Ways To Save Money

good enough. Then offer your services through your free, local newspaper.

Locksmith
There are many places where you can train to be a locksmith, even home study courses. I recommend you buy some books on starting your business and a book on creating a business plan. There are several free courses available online as well; you have to go and search for them. Purchasing books on marketing your business and the difference between a sole-proprietorship and a corporation would also be a good idea as well. Business start-up is a huge topic and much too complicated to go into. However, you must do some research and understand at least something about running a business before jumping in as being your own boss is not an ideal choice for everyone. The important thing to do is research and study business books first. Most businesses fail in the first five years because the person who starts it knows nothing about business. They hope to hang out their sign for goods or services and the money will come in. It never happens that way so you have to be realistic. You will need a plan and you should start small and pilot your business.

Medical Tests
It may not sound glamorous, maybe even scary, however it pays real money and the doctors do not ask any questions other than health-related ones. Currently, there are many medical studies going on around the country. These are not all for cancer or heart disease either. Somewhere, a company has a new product that heals scars quickly. They want people with scars who will try their product and let them photograph the results. Some company has a new tattoo removal system and they need people to

test it on. Some of these jobs are outpatient-type jobs where they pay you a few hundred pounds a month. Others are inpatient where you are kept in a hospital and monitored. These pay the most and may involve testing new drugs, anti-depressants or they may simply want to see how a healthy person reacts to an anti-inflammatory drug. You may even be one of the people who receive the placebo drug that does nothing and not the real drug. Check the Internet or if you have a local teaching hospital or research centre, they may be able to help too.

Recommended Jobs: Online Freelance Work
This is the best job for an ex-offender because it requires no background check, no drug tests, no psychological tests, no certifications or anything else. You are hired based on what you can do and nothing else matters. The only cost implication may be purchasing a laptop, or at the very least going to an Internet café.

I am talking about remote, work at home type jobs. Not the fake jobs you see on the Internet like those assemble-junk-at-home jobs or copying names from the phone book type jobs, as well as stuffing envelope jobs; those are all scams - there are no such jobs in existence. There is however, many legitimate work at home opportunities where small companies hire you online and pay up-front. These jobs may last a day, a week, or a month. You can work multiple jobs at once if you want or you can take a break or vacation anytime you want. If you only want to work one day a week, you can do it. You have complete control over how much you make and when you work and you never have to go to a job interview again.

If you are good with computers that help you secure

100 Ways To Save Money

work quicker, that will be an added advantage; however, it is not a necessity that you must have PC skills. These jobs vary depending on what the company needs. You work for one company for a few days, then work for another company. The jobs ranges from computer programming to data entry, webpage design, editing and proofreading, recording voicemail welcome messages, editing video, conducting web research, forum marketing, writing sales letters and anything else that can be done remotely. These jobs are posted on special Hire-Me Network sites by companies. You look through the listings and pick a job you want, and then tell the company what you want to be paid and when you can complete the job.

Delivery Driver
Many companies are willing to hire ex-offenders as delivery people as long as you have a clean driving record and no bans.

Join the Army
Joining the army means you can get paid and be educated at the same time. This is a rigorous process and you will have to pass many tests. You can find a link to the army policy on hiring ex-offenders on their websites.

Telephone Customer Service
Several companies exist that are willing to hire ex-offenders to handle phone-based customer service. There are also sales jobs that will do the same; this may or may not include a basic salary, and you may be paid only via a bonus scheme.

100 Ways To Save Money

Temp Agency
Temp agencies are a good option. You will have to explain what your conviction was for and convince them that it will not affect your work. Many companies that would never consider hiring an ex-offender full-time will hire people from a temp agency or even short-term contract people without a background check.

Family Business
You may be able to work in a family or friend's business. The point here is to be optimistic and look at all of your options. Be sure to offer a great service in their business and do not fall out over trivial disagreements.

Truck Driver
It is a myth that all trucking companies are willing to hire ex-offenders. It is also difficult because special licensing is required for larger trucks. If you are on parole, this kind of work may not be possible, because the job will likely require you to go out of town. If you are not on parole, then this would not be a problem. Truck driving jobs are not a sure thing and if you lack experience, it is unlikely you will be able to drive an 18-wheeler; maybe smaller trucks.

These are only a few of the listings available. You can find many agencies that specialise in helping ex-offenders find employment. Pre-plan your answer to the tough question like: "Have you ever been convicted?" During an interview, make sure you keep calm so that you are not immediately out of consideration.

100 Ways To Save Money

My Life Today

At first, I found it really difficult to find a job because I did not have any photographic ID, only my prison pass, which I was extremely embarrassed about. Presenting that to an employer would immediately indicate that I have a criminal record. In the meantime, I let several job opportunities pass me by so I could get my driver's licence in order to provide photographic identification. After I passed my driving test, I quickly started to apply for jobs and received many knock-backs. Some organisations would not even reply to my application form which upset me. This made me want to lie about having a criminal record in order to at least get to the interview stage. I also needed to obtain permanent accommodation to apply for a work which was another hassle.

Once I secured somewhere to live, which is a key aspect of getting into employment, I was then offered a job within the housing association to work with vulnerable, young people. I stayed in this place of employment for four years and gained a wealth of experience in customer relations and communication skills, group work and interacting with external partners. I had a burning hunger and ambition to succeed; you will need the same if you are to stay out of the clutches of the prison gates. You have to make a mental change to better your life, and when you get knocked down, rest, then and get back up again. Never give up or give in to old habits; the street does not need to keep you captive.

I was seconded over by Islington Council to set up and run the Islington Gang Disruption Team and to look after the threshold of young people from 16-25, because they were not able to engage with them as they were high level, active gang members. I

100 Ways To Save Money

gradually moved up the career ladder after setting up two of their witness protection programmes in South London. I met some really influential police officers along the way and had a top superintendent train me. He went on to be the Head of Security for the Olympics and the founder of the Black Police Association.

My message to you is clear, do not allow your past to dictate your future, and continue to strive for your goals because what is yours no one can take away from you or prevent you from achieving your goals. Just because you have been in prison does not mean you should allow any of your days be wasted. You have 24 hours in a day just like everyone else. Do your best to use those hours to achieve your goals and not allow any negative energy from people telling you that you cannot be a success, because tomorrow is never promised to anyone. I hope that I have inspired you to make lasting change for proactive success.

Good luck.

Gwenton Sloley
www.gwentonsloley.com

100 Ways To Save Money

Poem: Faces

My words emancipate the page
And scribe a freedom song
I was once shackled in my mind
With repression doing me an injustice
I moved beyond fearlessness to strive for excellence
My pen is heaven sent and now my trusted sword
I left top shotta's on the block
To U-turn my way to a legit outfit
Still street juices inside, I just contain it better in boardrooms
The streets bled my name and I got a wealth of repenting to do
Clothed in blu-ray paranoia
My life is widescreen cinematic view
Be the real deal, still finding my new feet
I do not want to jack his trainers
My Air Jordan trainers fit just fine
I have seen many burnt faces
With tear-stained traces
Wiping away the regret
I have a window of opportunity to climb into the next dimension
No longer a slave to the streets
I escaped perimeter mind-sets
Instead of getting perplexed
Over the curfew of freedom of speech
I seek out and promise to be a beacon of hope
The ones who listen with their hearts
Ended up in the grave
I had to listen to the gutter
To survive another day
For a moment, the pain of poor choices and consequences dampen my soul
Yet, I still made it out of the ghetto

100 Ways To Save Money

Traitorous words got me ducking and diving
I have forgotten how many fallen soldiers lay limp
To bring our fragmented community into alignment
Experience is the teacher of back together again
Offering comfort to the insane, who some refer to as deranged
Where I really want to be is just moments away
It is a perception of time and day
Time has no boundaries on the road to change
Money is their God and fame is their game
Where I really wanted to be was unearthed into the prime season of my life

100 Ways To Save Money

Coping with Redundancy

100 Ways To Save Money

Finally, I had found the job of my dreams; I worked for London Bubble Theatre Company in Bermondsey, South London, which was ideal for a drama queen like me! Every day I got to live, eat and breathe my passion. I would wake up feeling refreshed and grateful that I could live my purpose and get paid a fabulous salary of 20k plus per year. I felt like part of the team, I was valued and enjoyed my work-life for three years.

Prior to joining the London Bubble team in 2004, I was unemployed for nearly a year. I went through bouts of depression, not knowing why it was so hard to get a job and break into the creative arts industry.

Every time I stepped into the Job Centre, I felt inadequate and imagined that the person sitting on the other side of the desk looked down on me. After leaving my job in telecoms, which I hated with a passion, I decided it was best to do what I loved and nothing else. It was difficult making a career transition with no formal training, however, this time I wanted to make sure that I would be in a workplace where I felt appreciated.

A month before my interview with London Bubble, I was offered a job in Brixton Housing Association. However, the wage was £14,000 to manage their housing service projects. I asked them for an increase as the scale went up to £16,000 and they refused. I turned down the position because in my heart, I knew I was not being paid my worth and would only end up resenting them.

You have to understand that back in those days we were not going through a recession. Everything pertaining to the benefit system was different.

100 Ways To Save Money

However, to still live on a budget of Job Seeker's Allowance meant I could not afford the finer things in life. Due to me being long-term unemployed, I was placed in a specialist centre that would helped me update my CV, apply for jobs and assisted in filling out applications. When I came across London Bubble's 'Respect In Focus' post, I got my Theatre Practitioner friend, Tony Cealy, and Mark, former manager of the Salmon Youth Centre, to help me complete my application to the highest standard and create a workshop plan for the children. Finding a job for me was a group effort and I found the support useful. This time I was prepared to make sure I did a job I had an interest in and used all my creative skills of singing, drama and poetry.

The only thing I needed was a smart suit which of course I could not afford to buy. This is where Smart Works stepped in. As a long-term unemployed person, I was referred to them as per my tip number 96. Their team were lovely and made me feel welcomed. I had a two-hour appointment with them and came out feeling a million pounds. All of the above contributed to me securing my ideal job. Remember, looking for a job is a full-time job.

My contract with London Bubble was for three years and it was funded by Children In Need. Little did I realise that there was no additional funding to keep me on once my post came to an end. I was devastated when I found out I was being made redundant; I felt my world crumbling around me. It is such an uneasy feeling and in my head, alarm bells and panic stations were going off. I thought to myself, this was not fair age 28 and I was unsure about what it was I wanted to do next. I knew I loved to write so creating a book would be in the pipeline.

100 Ways To Save Money

London Bubble was really supportive about my transition. They offered me the option of being a self-employed Drama Workshop Facilitator, working part-time with them in the evenings. I thought to myself, this was a massive step; I had never been self-employed before, how would this work? I was courageous and ambitious enough to know that generating my own income would be the way forward, and for a while, it worked. I managed to secure an income of around £1,000 per month. However, I was never able to continuously bring in the freelance work or follow up on new leads for continued workshops. This was a downfall of mine and I had to learn the hard way.

The point that I am making here is although I was scared and upset about being made redundant, I was happy to know that I was creating a new path in business where I could be my own boss and the captain of my ship. Ultimately I would be a lot happier.

The quicker you get over the shock of realising that redundancy is real, the better equipped you can be to create an action plan for your next career move. If I had lacked that little push, I would have never become self-employed and moved on to establish my own publishing company: 'The Healing Factory Publications', and my own non-profit organisation: 'MPLOYME' that works with 16–24 year old young people who are in need of skills to get back into work. There is always a blessing in the storm if you wait long enough to see it.

Let me be honest with you, being self-employed is not for everyone. It takes a really strong character who does not mind walking alone at times. You miss many family gatherings and many lose many friendships along the way. This was my experience and I had to surround myself with positive people who understood my vision and did not get offended with a lack of communication on my part. The key point I am making here in this chapter is that redundancy does not define you. Do not allow the fear of not working to paralyse you. Instead, think fast about your back-up options that you can put into place until you can secure another job. The goal is to work at a job you love and never look back.

100 Ways To Save Money

Bonus: Crunch it Workbook

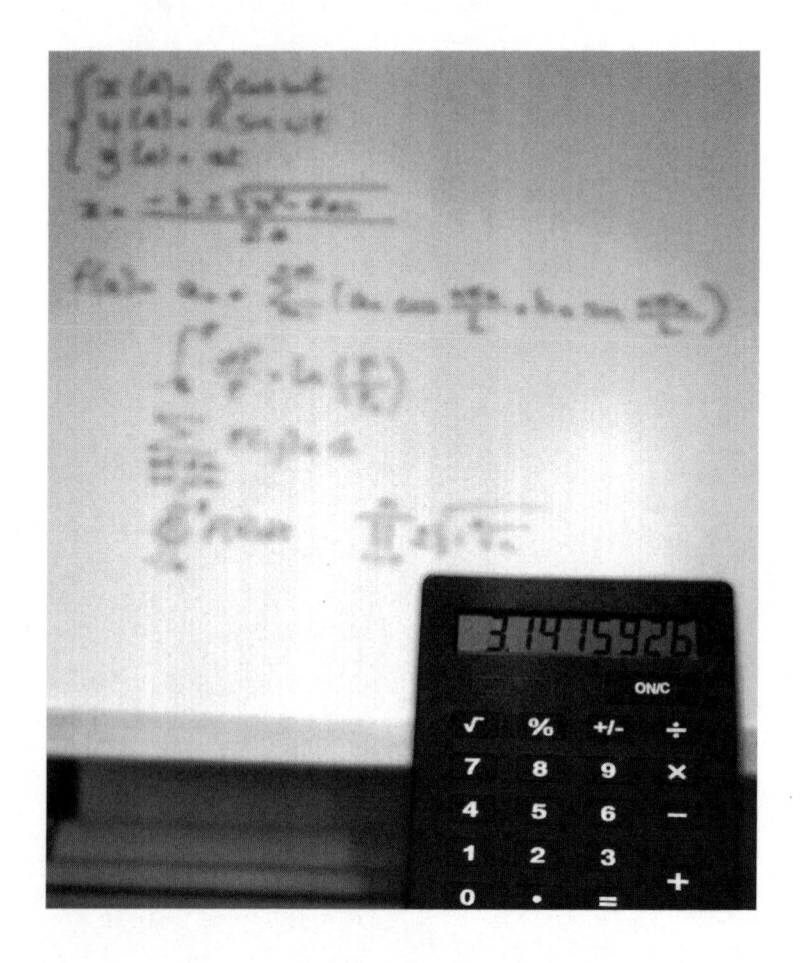

100 Ways To Save Money

As an additional bonus, I decided to create a special 'Crunch It' workbook to give you the practical tools to start the process of getting out of the hole that is the credit crunch and into employment. If you do the work in this section of the book, you can create a strategy that will ultimately help you escape the poverty mentality that so many of us are in bondage over.

This workbook belongs to:

....

By signing the declaration below, I am committed to taking on the responsibility of improving my employment prospects. I understand that I do not have to be a product of my environment. Change starts with a first step, and I boldly step forward to make improvements in my life for the better. My signature below shows my dedication and commitment in being proactive and breaking free from the chains of the recession.

Signed:..

Date: ....../....../......

100 Ways To Save Money

Crunch It Categories

1. Redundancy – The Final Call
2. Budgeting
3. Passive Income
4. Securing A Job
5. Goal Setting

Redundancy – The Final Call

The ground shakes under your feet as you and millions of others have faced the axe of redundancy. Here is your emergency plan to get you back on the right track. Remember the correct attitude is everything.

1. When you first found you were being made redundant, how did you feel?

I.felt……………………………………………………………………
………………………………………………………………………………
………………………………………………………………………………
………………………………………………………………………………
………………………………………………………………………………

2. Write down 5 words that best describes how you feel about your previous employer?

1…………………………………………………………………………
2…………………………………………………………………………
3…………………………………………………………………………
4…………………………………………………………………………
5…………………………………………………………………………

100 Ways To Save Money

3. Are you happy, sad or indifferent to being made redundant?......................................

4. Are you fearful about how you will pay your bills or take care of the family? (Please, explain your answer in depth below)

....
....
....
....
....
....
....

5. Are you scared you will not get another job? Yes/No (Please circle)

There are mixed emotions when being made redundant; it can create turbulence and uncertainty.

6. Write down 10 skill sets you can bring to a new job role? (e.g. strong administrative skills or you can touch-type 60 words per minute)

1..
2..
3..
4..
5..
6..
7..
8..
9..
10..

100 Ways To Save Money

Once you begin to unpack the burden that is redundancy, you can begin to look at your glass as half full. Now is the time to find a job that you are passionate about. Did you know that you spend over half your life at work? This means it is your responsibility to make sure you enjoy what it is you do.

Write a letter to your previous employers stating exactly how you are feeling? <u>DO NOT POST THIS LETTER TO YOUR PREVIOUS EMPLOYER.</u> This exercise is purely to help vent your frustration or relief about moving on and will help start the process of long-term change in your life.

Dear……………………………………

………………………………………………………………………………
………………………………………………………………………………
………………………………………………………………………………
………………………………………………………………………………
………………………………………………………………………………
………………………………………………………………………………
………………………………………………………………………………
………………………………………………………………………………
………………………………………………………………………………
………………………………………………………………………………

Yours faithfully,

……………………………………………

100 Ways To Save Money

Budgeting

Let us get down to the bones of it; the first step to getting a grip with your finances is to begin BUDGETING! It may be a challenge for those who have never done it before, but do not let that deter you. If you have reached this part of the book, then you should have completed the budgeting table in 'A Quick Guide To Financial Ordering and Basic Budgeting'.

1. Write down how frequently you would like to budget here. Is it on a weekly, every fortnight, or every monthly basis? : ………………………………………

2. Decide if you will write down your budget, use an Excel spreadsheet or make copies of the budget guide in this book………………………………………..….

Make sure you stick to your allocated budgeting timeslot and be disciplined about this. One thing about keeping budgeting records is that you have to be focused.

Your needs are essential items, your wants are things you would like but can live without. For example, if you would like a change of décor and a new carpet would help with this, write it down on your want list for when you can afford it in the future. Now, imagine if you have a tap pouring with money, what would you do, buy a car or a house? Dream big with no limitations and spend an hour on this and really put some thought into what you are about to write on your wish list. Think about your intentions behind the things you say and wants as well as the possibilities of receiving it. When you open your mind to how you will achieve this, your brain starts thinking of ways to bring your wants to you.

100 Ways To Save Money

Needs

"I need this item urgently"

100 Ways To Save Money

Wants

"If it is not broken, don't try and fix it"

100 Ways To Save Money

Wish list

"If money was no object, I would buy this"

....
....
....
....
....
....
....
....
....
....
....
....
....
....
....
....
....
....
....
....
....
....
....
....
....
....
....
....

100 Ways To Save Money

Questions:

3. What has prohibited you from previously budgeting?..
....
....
....

4. If you are currently budgeting, what motivates you to continue?

....
....
....

Complete these sentences:

5. I think budgeting is:

....
....
....

6. I find it hard to budget because:

....
....
....

7. I find it easy to budget because:

....
....
....

100 Ways To Save Money

8. I think money is
....
....
....

9. I fear money because:
....
....
....

10. I love money because:
....
....
....

11. How much is currently in your bank account?
....
....
....

I need you to pay attention and notice your responses as you write down theses sentences, and look at your negative thoughts and resistance as you go along. The idea is to start transforming your fears and negative thoughts into positive affirmations whilst taking massive action to improve your finances.

100 Ways To Save Money

Passive Income

<u>Definition of passive income:</u> A passive income is revenue received on a regular basis with little effort required to maintain it.

Tapping into your hobbies and creative passion means you will never have to work another day in your life. Imagine how fantastic that would be, to get up every morning with a new lease of life. The following are 9 top ways to earn money while you sleep:

1. **Royalties**
2. **Affiliate marketing**
3. **Investments**
4. **Real estate**
5. **Sell your services & products online**
6. **Start a freelance business**
7. **Network marketing**
8. **Flea markets**
9. **Participate in surveys and paid focus groups**

1. What do I love to do?
....
....
....

2. What hobbies would I like to do for free? (e.g. baking cakes or gardening)
....
....
....

100 Ways To Save Money

Note: Remember, if you are not yet certain about what you want to do as a career or what ignites your passion, you have to go out into the big, wide world and explore.

3. Make a list of 5 hobbies you have always wanted to try out?

Hobby 1
....

Hobby 2
....

Hobby 3
....

Hobby 4
....

Hobby 5
....

Give yourself six months to test which hobbies you like the best.

100 Ways To Save Money

Securing a Job

CV stands for Curriculum Vitae and serves as an overview of your employment history for potential employers. The purpose of a CV is to sell yourself and capture your potential employer's attention. You can embellish your CV but <u>never</u> tell lies. Go online and google a CV template which best suits you. If you have a fear of using computers, you need to get rid of that and become PC literate immediately. Get out of your comfort zone if you truly mean you want to make lasting changes. Unless you are a doctor or civil engineer, your CV needs to be 1–2 pages long.

1. Do you have a CV?

Yes/No (please circle)

2. When was the last time you updated your CV?..................................

Note: A CV should be updated every time you secure a new job, achieve educational qualifications, accreditations or attend a training course pertaining to your sector.

3. Write down 10 words that describes you in the working environment? (For example: focused, team player or punctual)

....
....
....
....

100 Ways To Save Money

....
....
....
....
....
....

4. Writing a Personal Statement and CV

A personal statement is the opening introduction of yourself in your CV; in this section you will write about your skills, abilities and character qualities. For example:

I am a highly organised individual who takes pride in my work. I work well in a team and perform well under pressure. I enjoy finding solutions to problems and attaining the best possible outcomes. I am motivated, focused and pay attention to detail. I am a self-starter or can work in a team. I am a creative thinker who gives valuable contributions and insight during meetings.

Using your 10 descriptive words, write your own personal statement here:

....
....
....
....
....
....
....

100 Ways To Save Money

....
....
....

You must have or learn to develop the following skills to help to secure a job:

- ✓ Good eye contact (not staring)
- ✓ Clean and tidy appearance
- ✓ Always be on time (call if you are going to be late)
- ✓ Ask questions in interviews and look interested
- ✓ Read up about company on their website
- ✓ Be professional at all times
- ✓ Speak standard English (no slang terminology)
- ✓ Let your personality shine
- ✓ Be confident
- ✓ Thank your potential employer for their time and smile

The following CV template is to help you create a professional CV that can at least get you to the interview stage. If you are feeling anxious here, do not worry, new ground is always going to be scary. Make sure you get a professional to go over your CV and give you constructive feedback before sending it out.

100 Ways To Save Money

CV Template

Your Name
Contact Details (including Town and County)
Telephone numbers including mobile contact details
Email address

PROFILE

KEY ACHIEVEMENTS

EMPLOYMENT EXPERIENCE

Dates of employment
Title Held, Name of Company
Dates of employment
Title Held, Name of Company
Dates of employment
Title Held, Name of Company

EDUCATION & TRAINING

CORE SKILLS

INTERESTS

REFERENCES AVAILABLE ON REQUEST

100 Ways To Save Money

It is time to move out of your comfort zone. I challenge you every month to learn new skills to move you out of the space in which you feel safe and secure. In order to be great, you have to stretch yourself and come out of your limiting mind-set and thoughts. It is not an easy road, however, it is rewarding and worth the effort.

Nothing is achieved by being *mediocre, only the strong survive. If you feel uncomfortable in interviews, you need to learn how to make eye contact and project your voice. If you are struggling to pay the bills, then you need an extra job or to set up a home business. The bottom line is, you have to make a proactive decision to be great. Now let's look at what is blocking you from the job or salary that you really require.*

What 5 obstacles are preventing you from being in a job you love or starting your own business?
1...
2...
3...
4...
5...

Now list 5 ways in which you can overcome these obstacles that are blocking you:
1...
2...
3...
4...
5...

100 Ways To Save Money

Make it a point to only think solution-based instead of focusing on what you do not have.

Goal Setting

Inspirational quote: The mind is like a parachute, it works best when open - Frank Zappa

We can sit down all day long talking about what we want to do and this and that. We will be foaming at the mouth saying we want to go left or right. However, how many of us really attained our goals? Do you even write down and commit to paper your heart's desires? Remember, your life is like a map and you have to plan which way you are heading or else you will get lost. In my Proactive Employment Workshops, I have created the following worksheet to assist participants on to the road of self-discovery.

1. Write down 3 achievable goals that you would like to attain for the following year:

Goal 1...
Goal 2...
Goal 3...

Now I want you to take an imaginative leap and visualise what your perfect day would look and feel like. Will you be waking up with joy beside the one you love or will all your bills be paid in advance? You need to be very specific here; remember, there are no limits, and be sure to dream big.

100 Ways To Save Money

2. My Perfect Day

3. Daily Personal Positive Mantra

You should make a point to have a positive mantra that you read out daily to yourself. It will help you get into the right state of mind to begin your day. Here is an example below to help you generate some ideas.

> "I am always striving for excellence. I expect only the best to follow my footsteps. I turn my dreams, aspirations and goals into reality. I am confident, intelligent and strong, and my grace is sufficient. I know and accept who I am and I love the skin I am in. I will use my voice to empower others on a global platform. I shape my destiny with positive, daily affirmations. Wherever I go and whatever I do, I always remember that success is a mind-set."

100 Ways To Save Money

Create Your Own Personal Positive Mantra below:

[   ]

4. On a scale of 1–10, rate the following questions. (1, being under-achieving and 10, excelling)

How satisfied are you with your life?

1..10

How successful are you in your career?

1..10

How good are you at writing out and achieving goals and targets?

1..10

100 Ways To Save Money

Code:

1-4 Needs urgent attention!!!
5-8 There is room for improvement.
9-10 Continue on your path, you clearly know where you are going.

5. In the next 3 months, what would you like to improve on? (e.g. time-keeping, job-hunting twice a week, and attending courses)

....
....
....
....
....
....
....
....
....
....
....

Now it is time to get serious. This time next year, it is your responsibility to make sure your life looks completely different than it does today. There is no point complaining about your circumstances and not doing anything to improve your situation. I get tired of hearing what folks say they are going to do; just be quiet and get on with it. You must now take this time to seriously create a 12-month projection plan of where you want to be in a year's time. You must take diligent action on a monthly basis. Please, do not feel overwhelmed at this stage, feel optimistic that you are planning your victory and mapping out your life.

Inspirational quote: If you fail to plan, you plan to fail – Benjamin Franklin

100 Ways To Save Money

12 Month Planner – Today's date: ….../….../…...

FIRST QUARTER OVERVIEW

January 20.... **Action points**	**February 20....** **Action points**	**March 20....** **Action points**

100 Ways To Save Money

Today's date: ...../...../.....

SECOND QUARTER OVERVIEW

April 20.... Action points	May 20.... Action points	June 20.... Action points

100 Ways To Save Money

Today's date: ...../...../.....

THIRD QUARTER OVERVIEW

July 20.... Action points	August 20.... Action points	September 20.. Action points

100 Ways To Save Money

Today's date: …../…../…..

FINAL QUARTER OVERVIEW

October 20…. Action points	November 20… Action points	December 20… Action points

Epilogue

The only way you are going to dig yourself out of the hole that is the credit crunch is to use a shovel. Heap up your worries, stress and debt to the left. Gently place reality, the truth and realism on the right. Make sure you dig deep to excavate the puss of negative thinking and be sure to scoop up your tears as it will help create a rainbow one day. Use your weeping to water your dreams of success. This too shall pass, even though the fridge may be empty, hard times are not going to last always. Better days are ahead for those who believe that they are not defined by their circumstances or environments.

Become a Change Agent and be driven to be the success story that you know you are. Be the one that got away from poverty's entrapment. When I tell people I am passionate about the credit crunch, I have met many snobs who look down their nose at me and other people who are less well-off than them. It is as though their money gives them the authority to be rude. I never want to disrespect another human being in that way. I do not care, I know what I am about and what message of hope I have been created to share. I have learned to have nerves of steel in those instances. This scenario is more about them than it is about you; ignore those negative, closed-minded people. Money or clothes does not maketh the man. Know your worth and know your value. You can have all the money in the world, but if you have ill health, you have nothing. I am talking from experience as the first edition of this book was written

100 Ways To Save Money

on my sick bed. I had a chest infection where I had difficulty breathing and thought my time on this earth was drawing to a close. I spent days in bed, bored out of my mind, feeling my life force slipping away from me. Then it dawned on me, what have I done with my life? And have I really left my mark? That night with the little frail energy I had, I got my laptop and typed up one small A4-size document that consisted of cost-effective tips. I planted a seed which went on to touch and help thousands of people. When you know your value is not defined by lining up in the Job Centre queue, you know a great deal.

I remember for a long while when being unemployed I always felt depressed when I had to sign on at Job Centre Plus; I was in receipt of £71.00 a week. It was the most humbling experience ever, especially as my self-employment status meant they deducted £22.00 per week. This meant I lived off £49.00 for six months. I was expected to earn the other £22.00 myself based on my last year's financial earnings. It was hard for me because I am dyslexic and found the copious amounts of form-filling tedious. I felt penalised constantly for having ambition, a business and trying to change my circumstances for the better, because Job Centre Plus calculated and averaged out my earnings based on my former year's tax return. Had it not been for the support of my family and friends, especially my mother, I would not have gotten through those dark days when I wanted to give up and simply quit.

Crying was my best friend and when the tears streamed down my face, my eyes would become puffed up and my teardrops would burn my face. You see, this is why I am passionate about working with the underdog. Not many people want to help the most vulnerable in the society; they prefer to stay away in favour of the elite caste system. The untouchables are human beings that eat, breathe and sleep, they deserve respect and dignity. As long as you have a drive to serve, you know that inner unction to make lasting change; you can impact your circumstances for the better. I want you to know you are victorious in every breath you breathe and only favour and fortune must know your name.

Okay, so you may have lost your job. It is not the end of the world, put it into perspective; rest if you must, dust off yourself and get back up into the race of life. The problem is not falling down, it is staying down. Winners never quit, quitters never win. Just keep on stepping boldly, putting one foot in front of the other. Bravely marching forth into your destiny, knowing deep within that better must come. You survived millions of your father's sperm to make it into this earthly plane; what a miracle you are. There must be a reason for your existence, a reason why you are still breathing. Figure out what you are here to do on this planet and ignite the passion within. Once you live in the purpose you were made for, you will never have to work another day in your life.

Since writing the first edition of this book in 2011, I became a film maker. I made three short films and one was about this book you are holding in your hands. It was called 'Money is too Tight to Mention' and was 15 minutes long. This film was aired on mainstream television via the Community Channel and broadcast on:

- BBC iPlayer
- SKY
- Virgin Media

- BT Vision

What is even more amazing is that I never paid a penny to make this film. Yes, you are reading correctly, it was done on no budget. This is why I keep hammering home about utilising your network and how worthwhile it can be. I performed at a charity event for Punch & Juicy, and I meant Joshua Harwood who had just graduated from university and wanted to build up his portfolio in film. I was delighted by this opportunity to work alongside him and have two films that were commercially viewed and available to watch on YouTube.

This book is my offering to be a part of the solution and to help you immediately ease the strain on your purse or wallet strings. My wish for you above all things is to remember to start thinking outside the parameters of your mind and to sharpen your life survival skills. My friends, the pinch will indeed become tighter, this is why you must be equipped and start implementing changes now. I hope you found warmth and humour in my candid way of expression. Remember, the only person that make a difference in your life is YOU! I have always found this scripture comforting during the good and bad days in my life:

"[11] I am not saying this because I am in need, for I have learned to be content whatever the circumstances. [12] I know what it is to be in need, and I know what it is to have plenty. I have learned the secret of being content in any and every situation, whether well fed or hungry, whether living in plenty or in want".

Philippians 4: 11-12 (NIV)

100 Ways To Save Money

I leave you with my poetical thoughts which summarises my feelings at this point in time.

Poem: Carry on, a change is coming

Within the racing heart of the financial turbulent storm
Keep on beating the historic drum of a healing, positive change
The deficit thunder may scream the loudest and leave you shaking in terror
You must remember your mighty warrior roar
Prowl the ice-blue skies of transformation
Learn to fly beyond your conditioned mental boundaries
Your magnificence will keep you dry when the bills are showering down
Stand firm, for this tempestuous time shall pass
The challenging times will become spiritual muscles that make you robust
Wear your battle scars with pride
Build on steel foundations by arming yourself with infinite knowledge
Never let your impoverished circumstance define who you are becoming
You are the bridge over a raging, repressed sea
The light in the wilderness of a bankrupt, snake-pit jungle
You are the backbone of the best you that we all anticipate to see
You can make it through your bleakest hour, if only you seek to believe in the Promised land

Lyrically Yours, Winsome 'Lyrical Healer' Duncan.

About the Author

Winsome Duncan's Biography

Overview
Winsome Duncan is an award-winning Social Entrepreneur. She has over two decades of experience teaching in workshops to disaffected, young people at risk. Winsome is passionate about empowering people in the wider community to access

opportunities and develop the necessary skills to enhance their socio-economic outcomes.

Background
Winsome Duncan is also known in her artistic capacity as 'Lyrical Healer' and she has had the pleasure of performing in the Houses of Parliament, Barclays Headquarters, Arsenal/Millwall football stadiums and the Royal Festival Hall. Her creative arts company 'The Healing Factory' has produced four books with her latest title *'100 Ways To Save Money'*.

Winsome Duncan has worked with young people who have special educational needs, in Pupil Referral Units, Young Offenders Team and the Lambeth Metropolitan Police Summer Holiday Projects. Coming from a background in the creative arts sector, Winsome utilises her creative skills to incorporate in her employability workshops. She uses her innovative trademark style and artistic talents as a tool to educate, inspire, empower and motivate her clients and young people to explore avenues for personal self-development. This is achieved through her unique style of engagement, and she uses the disciplines of song, poetry and film-making. Winsome is an accredited mentor and a Desmond Tutu Peer Mentor. Winsome has a second company called MPLOYME which is a not-for-profit organisation that specialises in Proactive Employment Workshops.

Specialisms
- Strategic Planning
- Proactive Employment Empowerment
- Youth Employability

100 Ways To Save Money

Film Maker
As a film maker, Winsome's short films *'The Healer In Me'* and *'Money's Too Tight to Mention'* have appeared on:
- BBC iPlayer
- SKY
- Virgin Media
- BT Vision

Haiti A Vision Of Hope was filmed entirely on her camera phone.

Unique Selling Point of Business
- Workbook: 100 Ways To Conquer The Credit Crunch
- Using the creative arts as a medium to educate, inspire and empower
- Fusing creative arts to make learning enjoyable and memorable using audio visual and kinaesthetic tools

Clients include:
- Charities (that work with unemployed, young people, ex-offenders and vulnerable clients)
- Corporate companies with staff at risk of the 3r's; redundancy, redeployment and are re-applying for their roles

Accolades and Achievements:
- Ixion Challenger Gold Award 2014
- Southwark Arts Forum Award – Best Emerging Talent 2013
- Southwark Culture Award 2007
- Accredited Mentor and Desmond Tutu Peer Mentor
- Level 2 & 3 Principals of Business and Administration

Ixion Challenger Gold Award

On Tuesday 3rd July 2014, I attended the Ixion Enterprise Awards at Westminster Hall, London. My company MPLOYME was nominated for the Challenger Award. This award was for businesses that demonstrated tenacity in overcoming obstacles. I attended the ceremony with my mother and we were welcomed by a buffet lunch and networking.

After lunch, we entered the hall and were warmly greeted by Ixion staff and the ceremony commenced. There were silver and gold awards given to each category. When it came to mine, my heart began to beat rapidly. I squeezed my mother's hand tightly and said a small prayer. Then the Chairman, Adam Sharples, said "The winner of the Challenger Gold Award goes to Winsome Duncan."

The room stopped, time stood still and, as I rose up out of my chair, everything became slow motion. I could feel the emotions bubbling up inside of me. 'I won' I thought. I felt so proud of myself and all the hard work that had gone into the building of my company, MPLOYME.

Ixion Holdings was instrumental during the process of me becoming full-time in my business. Their business advice has helped me to expand the vision of this book you hold in your hands into a series of Proactive Employment Workshops. The New Enterprise Allowance financial assistance has contributed to the making of *100 Ways To Save Money*. I have been able to tell my story of living on a low wage and how I turned my life around using my gifts and talents. I will be forever grateful to these programmes that inspire enterprising ideas to flourish.

You, the reader, must never give up on your goals or dreams. Always know that you are destined for greatness, and it is imperative that you continue on your journey. Fear must never be in your *vocabulary;* walk with the boldness of a pack of lions. Protect your dreams fiercely and, most of all, wake up excited to start the day.

Services

Winsome Duncan is available for bookings in the areas of:

- Corporate consultancy redundancy packages
- Motivational seminars and conferences
- Special guest appearances
- Employability workshops
- Staff inset training
- Keynote Speaker
- Master classes

In the first instance, please email us with your enquiry: mploymerecruitment@hotmail.com

MPLOYME

Our mission statement: To educate individuals through training and development to improve their employment prospects, budgeting skills and self-confidence.

MPLOYME is a not-for-profit organisation that specialises in the following areas:

- Corporate consultancy redundancy packages
- Master Classes | Conferences | Seminars
- Annual Networking Enterprise Job Fair
- Proactive Employability Workshops

ABOUT MPLOYME
There are many people experiencing financial hardship during the current economic downturn. Basic expenses such as paying fuel bills, purchasing food, clothing, paying rent and mortgages are real struggles faced by many families. Even those who are working are unable to meet many of their priority bills and are getting into serious debt with the risk of losing their homes.

Unemployment is a very real situation for many people in the UK and worldwide. Whether this has been as a result of redundancy, sickness, or the end of short-term contracts, the outcome is very real for people who now find themselves caught in the poverty trap.

100 Ways To Save Money

Government efficiency measures and legislative changes have impacted on benefit entitlement in the United Kingdom which has left many individuals living on a reduced income and having to move out of social housing that they are no longer able to afford. MPLOYME works with:

- 16-24 year-olds who are NEET (Not in Education, Employment or Training)
- The unemployed
- Single parents
- Organisations who require corporate consultancy redundancy packages and staff development to make them efficient in supporting the above client groups

To contact us, please visit our website: www.mployme.org

RMClarke Photography

Behind The Lens

Richard Macien Clarke is a London-based commercial photographer specialising in portraits and business photography for individuals and corporate clients looking for professional, creative and tailored images.

Born in Haiti, Richard grew up in Paris and has been working in London for over a decade. For more information, visit: www.rmclarkephotography.com

Contact Us

We would like to hear your valuable feedback about *'100 Ways To Save Money'*. Contact Winsome 'Lyrical Healer' Duncan through her networks:

Websites: www.mployme.org
www.creditcrunchqueen.com
www.lyricalhealer.co.uk

LinkedIn: Winsome Duncan
Facebook: Winsome Duncan
Facebook pages:
www.facebook.com/mployme
www.facebook.com/TheLeadingLadiesClub
www.facebook.com/authorwinsomeduncan

Twitter: lyricalhealeruk
Wordpress: www.lyricalhealer.wordpress.com
YouTube: www.youtube.com/lyricalhealer
MySpace: www.myspace.com/lyricalhealer
Sound Cloud: www.soundcloud.com/lyricalhealer

Useful Links

Pecan Foodbank
www.*pecan*.org.uk

Money Advice Service
www.moneyadviceservice.org.uk

Citizens Advice
www.citizensadvice.org.uk

Experian
www.experian.co.uk

National Debt Line
www.nationaldebtline.co.uk
0808 808 4000

One In Four
www.oneinfour.org.uk
0208 697 2112

Samaritans
www.samaritans.org
08457 90 90 90

Talk To Frank
www.talktofrank.com

Study Notes

100 Ways To Save Money

Study Notes

....
....
....
....
....
....
....
....
....
....
....
....
....
....
....
....
....
....
....
....
....
....
....
....
....
....
....

100 Ways To Save Money

100 Ways To Save Money